SHARE YOUR PALE.
BUILD YOUR BF ... M.

LIFESTYLE
MILLIONAIRE

AKIRA IGUCHI

NASHVII

LIFESTYLE MILLIONAIRE

© 2017 Akira Iguchi

Published in New York, New York, by Morgan James Publishing. Morgan James and The Entrepreneurial Publisher are trademarks of Morgan James, LLC. www.MorganJamesPublishing.com

The Morgan James Speakers Group can bring authors to your live event. For more information or to book an event visit The Morgan James Speakers Group at www.TheMorganJamesSpeakersGroup.com.

ISBN 978-1-68350-190-9 paperback
ISBN 978-1-68350-191-6 casebound
ISBN 978-1-68350-192-3 eBook
Library of Congress Control Number: 2016913874

Cover Design by:
Alan Dino Hebel
www.bookdesigners.com

Interior Design by:
Megan Whitney
Creative Ninja Designs
megan@creativeninjadesigns.com

In an effort to support local communities, raise awareness and funds, Morgan James Publishing donates a percentage of all book sales for the life of each book to Habitat for Humanity Peninsula and Greater Williamsburg.

Get involved today! Visit
www.MorganJamesBuilds.com

Thank you to my Mother, Father and all the people

that kept believing in me throughout my life.

— Akira

TABLE OF CONTENTS

INTRODUCTION

MEET THE LIFESTYLE MILLIONAIRES, A NEW CLASS OF WEALTHY ENTREPRENEURS

Would you like to wait until retirement to start enjoying your life? Does the thought of making money while working from a tropical paradise make you want to run back into your cubicle?

Would you like your obituary to read, "Employee Number 176505. Never broke any rules. Always asked for permission. Successfully ignored all passions, personal talents, and desire to live an exceptional life. Legacy: N/A."

If you answered "yes" to any of these questions, please don't spend any more of your valuable fifteen-minute water break allowances reading this book.

If you answered, "no" to all three questions, you belong among a new class of wealthy individuals who spend their days turning their passion into paychecks while helping others.

1

They do what they want, when they want, where they want, and with whom they want.

The Lifestyle Millionaire model is not for scammers or those who want to bank and bolt. It's not about compensating for hurt egos or shaming others.

Instead, Lifestyle Millionaires see their financial success as an indication of how many individuals they've impacted and how many lives they've revived.

To Lifestyle Millionaires, money means access, it means impact, and it means living their days aligning their precious resources and priorities with whom and what they love.

These are Lifestyle Millionaires. A new class of wealthy entrepreneurs. If this lifestyle sounds like your dream, you're in the right place.

Read on.

WHY LIFESTYLE MILLIONAIRES ARE POISED TO DOMINATE THIS GENERATION

Advice like "Graduate, get a secure job, work nine to five until age sixty-five, then retire and do what you love" has always seemed worthless in my eyes.

When people justified that this approach was "secure," I wondered how they still got laid off. When they told me it was "predictable," I couldn't seem to understood why I would work a "predictable" job I hated simply because it predicted that I would be doing that same painful job for decades to come. When they told me they would rather get paid less than have to go it on their own without knowing how much they'd make, I wondered how guaranteed pennies were more valuable to them than potential millions.

Luckily, now I am no longer the only one questioning such age-old wisdom.

With the rapid advancement of technology, we can connect with people thousands of miles away in seconds, raise our voices to join a global discussion, and discover almost anything we want to learn from the comfort of our very own couch.

With such potential and lucrative payouts, others are joining me in asking why they need to "pay their dues" before getting paid well, why they need to work bland jobs totally disconnected from their passions, and why they can't make an incredible living changing lives and sustaining their lifestyle from their laptop while sitting on a tropical beach.

It was from these questions that I began my search for a business model that would allow me to:

- do what I love
- buy what I like
- live where I want
- make a massive impact and
- contribute to society

The Millionaire Lifestyle business model is the answer to that search and my self-made eight-figure income.

I call this book *Lifestyle Millionaire* because these days it is possible to make a very profitable business starting with only your lifestyle and passion. Look at Starbucks and other Internet-providing cafés. You will find the same people there day after day typing away on their computers or texting on their phones. Is it just because they like the coffee and the atmosphere? Not entirely. Actually, that café is their office. Many of these individuals, if they are not already wealthy, are building wealth without an office, without furniture, without borrowing money, without employees, and without sophisticated technical skills. They are independent businesspersons, controlling their own time, money, calendar, contacts, and resources.

The truth is, the world today is very different from the world of just ten years ago. You can start with nothing and learn almost anything online. Everyone starts somewhere, and today it's as if Google awaits your every request for information. YouTube and Kindle-type e-readers are there to help you, like instructors you don't have to pay. You can literally start with nothing more than yourself, your intelligence, and your passion. That passion is your greatest resource—and you already have it, or the makings of it. My own story will show how you can follow, believe in, and coach others on your passion so that everyone profits.

Life coaching itself is the other part of this opportunity. Coaching will continue to grow as an industry because as stress intensifies its impact on individuals, they will need help and support not only to keep their lives on track and realize their goals but also to find satisfaction and fulfillment in their lives. You will read much more about this tension in this book, but for now it is enough to say that this is a great time to build a coaching business from practically nothing more than a good cell phone.

Coaching as an industry has a great future. Soon it will no longer be considered exotic or only for the rich and famous. It will be as common as personal training is today. Technology will provide coaches with excellent options for coaching their clients internationally, but local in-person connections will continue to be important as technology continues to integrate online with offline. Coaching will be delivered via computers, smartphones, and other mobile devices. Coaching has also outgrown its early dependence on certification. By qualifying your coaching through the outcomes of your passion, you can outpace the competition and become an authority in your field. The online world awaits you. You can start a blog and attract clients as you provide life-enhancing tips to followers. You can publish an e-book on your passion or create a YouTube segment that imparts the know-how viewers crave.

Do you have a passion for something? Do you have a burning desire to make something happen as a result of that passion? Specifically, have you always wondered how you could turn that passion into a profitable business? Wonder no longer! The Lifestyle Millionaire Coaching model was created precisely to answer these questions. This book will show you how you can apply the principles and practices that have brought me to the success I enjoy today. Even if you are not sure what your passion is, these pages will give you the guidance and structure you need to pursue and discover it. My book will show you not only how to identify, pursue, and develop the passion that is yours by nature, it will also show you how to translate that passion into a coaching business that creates profit for you and others. By putting my steps and strategies into practice, you, too, can realize your own success!

What is a Lifestyle Millionaire Coach? It is a person who has been trained to build a business around their passion by training other people to do the same. If that sounds complicated, it will become clear as we proceed. Basically, we are talking about a "ripple effect" here. That's why everything I tell you as your coach, about identifying your passion and using it as a basis for building a profitable coaching business, you should not only follow and do but also apply to your own coaching clients. Sometimes I'll be saying that you should do such and such, while other times I'll say your clients should do it. For all intents and purposes, these terms are interchangeable. Why? Because what you learn to do in this book is also what you will be training your own clients to do as future coaches themselves.

How profitable can a Lifestyle Millionaire Coaching business become? Well, by using the same process I will describe for you in this book, I have been able to enjoy an eight-figure yearly income. My seven books, including *Power Talk* and *Power Nomad,* have sold over 200,000 copies in Japan, Korea, and Taiwan. This has all come about as a result of my passion for helping others to lead more fulfilling lives. In my eyes, my greatest personal achievement has been helping more than 100,000 people change their lives for the better over the past ten years.

When you read those last two sentences, do they ring a bell with you? I ask because the Lifestyle Millionaire Coaching model contained in this book is intended for individuals seeking the satisfaction of making a positive difference in the lives of others while simultaneously prospering themselves. Are you that individual? If so, you have the right book in your hands.

As you read, you will encounter episodes of my own personal story appearing at frequent intervals. Hopefully, these anecdotes will inspire and motivate you through the personal insights as we explore the book's key lessons and how you can make them work for you.

If you're unsatisfied with your current job, life situation, or the state of your entrepreneurial project, you're in the right place.

Ask yourself, are you being paid what you're worth? Often, the salary you get is in direct proportion to how much contribution you make to another's life. I know you work hard. But how much of your time and energy is spent on low-return tasks like large group meetings, protocol training, paper shuffling, etcetera?

I'm about to show you a business method that can allow you to spend your time working on your passion, changing lives, and getting paid for your contribution and impact, not how many meetings you attended or papers you shuffled.

The only remaining question is...

Are you ready to begin your Lifestyle Millionaire journey?

CHAPTER ONE

WHAT IS YOUR PASSION?

I have said that this book is about your passion. What is a passion? Far more than interest or excitement, a passion is a compelling enthusiasm or deep desire for something. Passions are inclinations and desires carried to a high degree of intensity. When you are deeply passionate about something, that thing draws you, consumes you; it's never far from your thoughts. You have a commitment to it, an abiding relationship with it; you want to know all you can about it.

What does this book have to do with passion? The answer is that your passion or natural bent or inclination is the starting point for building on the model of business success the book is all about. The business plan you will read about starts with the person who is reading about it: you. Rather than asking you to conform to some general, one-size-fits-all plan, we start with what is *natural and right already for you*—your passion. That's why the first key to the success in following this plan is to . . .

"BE WHERE YOU ARE, OTHERWISE YOU WILL MISS YOUR LIFE."

BUDDHA

Does this rule seem simple or obvious? Simple it may be, but it definitely is not obvious. Why else would most people start their search for enterprise by looking to see what and who else is out there? Look around you. Virtually everything you see, hear, feel, taste, and touch is there because of the ideas and efforts of others.

Of course, this pertains to the matter of work and livelihood as well. Few people start out working for themselves. Instead, they look for jobs created by others. So it is tempting to wonder, "Where is my place? Where do I fit in?" Unless you have had a parent, teacher, coach, or friend who strongly advised you to look within yourself for direction—to listen to your own mind, to decide what you wanted and go after it—you have likely tended to follow the example set by those around you and looked "out there" to know where you were going. If you did not have such an influence, consider this book as such a guiding voice, and ponder the rule—the one that is simple but not so obvious—*to begin where you are.*

As you read my story, you will see that I tended to make that same assumption, implicit in the lives of those around me, that it was proper to listen to others' voices. Also, as you will see, that outward direction did not work for me.

My rise to the top wasn't easy.

Like many people who have created their own success on their own terms, my ambition was born out of adversity. When you think of the world's top leaders and innovators, they're usually not people who were born rich or who were the most popular in school or even who played by all the rules in life. They're people who thought a little differently, who wanted something more, who were a bit of an outsider marching to their own drum, but who always knew that somehow, some time, someway, they would succeed on their own terms. The question was, how?

When I was a teenager growing up in Japan, I had a very difficult time. I didn't fit in to the culture of conformity. The kids that did were quick to fall in line, to go along with the crowd, to be agreeable, friendly, and mild. I was different—outspoken, opinionated, with hardly a care about what other people thought. It wasn't that I was uncaring. I just wanted to say what I wanted to say and do what I wanted to do. I was naturally free spirited. Alas, in Japan being free spirited spelled disaster, socially.

I was the nonconforming bird in school, and so the pecking began, first as teasing, and finally as brutal bullying. It became so bad that I ended up changing schools a total of five times between middle and high school.

Perhaps as you read this part of my story you were wondering: What has this to do with passion? The answer is one of the most powerful ways to find your passion: struggle. Ask yourself:

- How have I struggled in life?
- When were things really difficult for me?
- What was I up against?
- How did I overcome it?

The last question is the clue, for in overcoming the difficulty you opened the way to a new phase of your life. I will shortly be suggesting other ways to find your passion, but the first one is to look at that for which you have fought and conquered.

A POSSIBILITY IN TIME

We will shortly return to the subject of finding your passion—which you now know is the place to "begin where you are." Meanwhile, I will ask you to consider building a business on your passion. Perhaps this is the first time you are being asked to consider taking what you have long been passionate about and making it into a business. How would that work? Let's consider an example.

Suppose your passion is holistic health. You are interested—no, you are *passionate!*—about the subject. You read up on it, you follow its principles of diet, exercise, and holistic medicine to keep yourself healthy. You even talk about it with friends and family, seeking to interest them in following a course of right eating, etc., that a philosophy of holistic health prescribes.

But have you ever thought of yourself as a professional coach in the field of holistic health? Have you ever entertained the thought that your passion could have some earning potential, that you could use your know-how about this rich subject to attract clients who would pay you to coach them in learning and following what you have gleaned by focusing your attention in this field? Or perhaps, instead of health, your passion is birds, or flying, or art, or travel. Whatever it is, can you begin to entertain the possibility of turning that passion into a Lifestyle Millionaire Coaching business?

ENTREPRENEURSHIP: A GROWING TREND

Entrepreneurs are individuals who identify a change that needs to happen and who realize that they are the ones who need to bring that change forward. In my early twenties I became passionate about being a pioneer—one who opens the way for an enterprise to take root and grow.

In my first year as a college student in America, I had become excited about the personal growth movement that was taking place in this country. When I returned to Japan, I realized that the movement had not really taken off in a similar way there. So I determined to be the instigator, the one who lights a match to start a conflagration that would sweep across my homeland as it was sweeping across the United States.

A report sponsored by Babson College and Baruch College finds that 27 million working-age Americans—a record high of nearly 14%--are starting or running new businesses. A growing number of people consider entrepreneurship an attractive career option. Fifty-one percent of the working population believes good opportunities for starting businesses exist, the first time that figure has risen above half. So if you think it may be time for you to take your passion to the next level, you are in good company.

CLARIFYING YOUR PASSION

If you are to consider building a business around your passion, it follows that you need to be crystal clear about what that passion is. How clear are you about your passion? Perhaps you are so sure about what it is that it came immediately to mind as you read the above description of a passion. On the other hand, maybe you're not quite sure what your passion is. If that is the case, read on.

There are certain indicators that help identify a passion, even in its formative state. As you read the following part of my early life story, you will see that I did not know what my passion was. Nevertheless, the seed of that passion was already there in me. See if you can discern, even through the difficulties describe, the germ of a desire that might lead eventually to my passion.

At an early age, I may not have known what my passion was, but I certainly knew what my passion was not: conformity. For as long as I can remember, I have been unreservedly opposed to following standard patterns of thought and action. Nonconformity was, and still is, *a natural inclination* of mine. I never set out to be a rebel; it's just that every time I try to follow the pack, something inside me tells me to stop. Even at this early stage, I was unable to fit the model, unwilling to fall in line, and unprepared to behave like everyone else. This marching to my own drum has caused me a lot of pain and suffering.

That was before I learned how to use it to my advantage.

PASSION INDICATORS

There are several indicators you can use to better discern your passion. Let's look at five of them now: investment, inclination, dream, motivation, and giving.

1. The Investment Indicator

When I started my pioneering efforts in Japan, I spent a lot of time examining people's interests. I asked, "What are people passionate about?"

Right away, I noticed a strong, widespread interest in learning English. I went to bookstores to see how many books there were on the subject and how many people were buying them. These customers were also investing in classes and tutors to learn and practice spoken English.

You can use this same indicator to determine your passion. Simply ask yourself: *What is it that I have spent money, time, and energy on in my life?*

Whatever the answer, it must be more than a passing fancy or even a strong interest. Look for investment over longer periods of time to help weed out short, intense interests that may not actually be your passion.

2. The Inclination Indicator

Another way to identify your passion is by looking at your own natural inclinations or directions you have been drawn toward over a longer period of time. Think of these inclinations as currents carrying your attention and energy in a certain direction. If something has long captured your interest, it may well be an indicator of your passion.

The following activity may help you begin to discover or rediscover your passion by highlighting some natural inclinations and bringing you clarity. If you already are clear about your passion, doing the activity can still increase your precise understanding of it.

Activity: Natural Inclinations

What have people always said are your talents? Natural inclinations are different from skills. They are predispositions or fondness for certain subjects or experiences, often since childhood but they could also be discovered later on.

Directions: Look over the list below. Write down the items that describe you. Add your own items to the list.

discernment	communicating	writing	speaking
acting	drawing	music	singing
drama	marketing	team player	loner
leading	caregiving	coaching	helping
listening	organizing	traveling	storytelling
sports-inspiring	entertaining	healing	teaching
guiding	innovating	brainstorming	using numbers
managing details	tasting	orchestrating	planning
designing	understanding	dreaming	exercising
laugh	games	smiling	being happy
comforting	executing plans	making people	cooking
thinking outside the box		seeing the best in people	

_____

_____

As you read one or more of the items above, many may have made you instantly say, "That's me!" Perhaps one term even jumped out at you. Natural inclinations can act as corridors to lead you to your passion.

3. The Dream Indicator

Still another way to identify your passion is to think about your answer to the question, *"What is my dream?"* Everyone has some cherished aspiration of what could transpire in the best possible situation. What vision have you nurtured about being, having, or doing something that would bring fulfillment to your life?

Perhaps you've thought of those visions as just dreams, something unattainable. Having a dream doesn't just mean entertaining a fantasy. It means engaging with your highest aspiration. When you picked up this book, though, you took a step toward making your dream a reality. Write it down below or on a separate paper. And remember, *writing*—not just thinking about our dreams—is important because it forces us to commit to in actual words a notion that perhaps has previously been vague or not fully understood.

MY DREAM IS _____

As you may have found just now, the act of putting your dream into words not only makes it concrete but also strengthens it. Writing down your dream gives it life, makes it appear more possible and realistic than before.

Besides writing down your dream, another way to add reality to it is to communicate it to another person. Tell someone about your dream. When you do, important things can happen: that person will not only understand your dream, they can also appreciate it, share your enthusiasm for it, and may even want to help you achieve it.

4. The Motivation Indicator

By now, you should be clear that your passion, by its very nature, is a strong emotion. It is having fire in your belly, a burning desire that yearns for fulfillment. It is not something merely to think about but to experience to the fullest. What is the vital ingredient to transform your passion into a successful achievement for you? Motivation.

In the next episode of my story, you will learn that for a time in my life, my motivation was little more than a spark. Thankfully, it had not gone out. There was still hope.

As a teenager, I watched kids going about their normal lives with academic success and all the regular stuff that teens enjoy: having friends, hanging out, enjoying high school activities, and having girlfriends.

By contrast, during that time of my life, I felt so alone, isolated, and painfully inferior. I was grateful to have my parents, but they couldn't be with me throughout my school days.

I continued to live a solitary existence of admiring other teenagers laughing in groups at restaurants. And there I was, standing alone outside with my face pressed against the window, wondering what their lives must be like. I wondered how I'd ended up with such a sad, lonely life. I hadn't made any plans for after graduation.

Even in that emotional state, there was still a tiny fire deep inside of me. Despite all evidence to the contrary, in my heart, I knew that the failed, isolated teen I had become was not who I really was.

Inside, I was raw and hurt. I spent all my spare time at home, isolated and alone. Even though I was profoundly unhappy, I had a tiny flame inside me that always believed I could be something more. My mom, a devout Christian, always reminded me: no matter how bleak things seem at the moment, there is always hope.

5. The Giving Indicator

The last place I recommend looking to brainstorm or discern your passion is in areas in your life where you already volunteer, share freely, or give of your resources. This is a category many people reference when they say things like, "Choose a career where you can do the work you would do even if nobody paid you for it."

Where in your life do you already add value or contribute without compensation? For example, are you a volunteer ski instructor, caretaker at the public gardens, or guide at a museum?

To look at it another way, ask yourself, "If money were not a factor, how would I spend my time?" Be sure to choose something that is sustainable and fulfilling when answering this question, not just a hedonistic fantasy. Many people presume that if money were not a factor, they'd spend their days drinking on a private island and watching live sporting events until they fall asleep in a hammock, wake up the next morning, and start the whole routine over.

Often that ritual is great for a week, maybe a month, but by the end of eight weeks, unless you're a true aficionado, that life becomes incredibly dull. Ask any individual who raced to retirement and within their first year came back onboard as a consultant. "The stuff I used to do to relax was only fun as a break from my work, from the things that engaged and excited me. When partying was my whole life, all the fun went away and it became incredibly boring" is usually their explanation. This situation is why I encourage you to uncover your passion by examining areas where you already "work for free," not scenes from movies you fantasize reliving.

Now that we've discussed you and your passion, I want to bring your attention to another important motivator that is often overlooked or ignored entirely in business: "enlightened selfishness." This could be described as motivation to help others as a means to helping yourself. Unlike greed or manipulation, which focuses on using others to get what you want, enlightened selfishness asks, "How can I achieve my dreams by making another person's dreams come true?"

Enlightened selfishness is based on a truth about human nature and a key component of the Lifestyle Millionaire's passion-based business plan. Perhaps you have experienced how making a positive difference in someone else's life can make you happy. The Lifestyle Millionaire Coaching model is predicated on that same concept of achieving your goals as an outcome of coaching others on how to get what *they* want.

Every time you employ this method's principles and practices to help someone else get ahead, you are growing and benefiting yourself. The Lifestyle Millionaire Coaching method is also a form of self-perpetuating job security because the more your clients realize how sincerely you want to help them succeed, the more frequently they will want coaching and recommend others to you.

Furthermore, Lifestyle Millionaire Coaching as a business is often more sustainable because it feeds your own passion and applies your interests in the process of helping others.

Having covered indicators for passion such as investment, inclination, dreams, motivators, and giving, where are you in terms of discovering and following your passion? Use the activity below to provide greater clarity.

How Motivated Are You?

Directions: Uncover your current status by choosing the numbers below that best describe your awareness in, dedication to and investment in your passion.

Key: 1 = Not at all; 2 = somewhat; 3 = moderately; 4 = very much; 5 = completely

1. I am fully aware of my passion.   1 2 3 4 5

2. I am able to speak knowledgably about my passion. 1 2 3 4 5

3. I can effectively teach others about my passion.   1 2 3 4 5

4. My passion enables me to inspire others.   1 2 3 4 5

5. I am dedicated to success.   1 2 3 4 5

6. I am able to persist through difficulties.   1 2 3 4 5

7. I am easily discouraged.   1 2 3 4 5

8. I need help to overcome my current situation.   1 2 3 4 5

9. I am investing in my passion daily, monthly.   1 2 3 4 5

10. I hang around people who encourage my passion.   1 2 3 4 5

11. I have a plan for barriers inhibiting my passion.   1 2 3 4 5

12. I know how to get what I need most now.   1 2 3 4 5

13. I am enthusiastic about my passion.   1 2 3 4 5

14. Others know about my passion and expertise.   1 2 3 4 5

15. I mostly ignore my passion.   1 2 3 4 5

16. My passion is never far from my thoughts.   1 2 3 4 5

If you were unclear before about what passion you can turn into a Lifestyle Millionaire Coaching business, perhaps by now you have gained some clarity. Even if you don't feel fully ready, try identifying one passion now and working from there. You can always come back and choose something else. However, as you know from reading maps, it's hard to know where to go if you don't know where you are now.

MY PASSION IS _____

ARTICULATING YOUR PURPOSE

If you were to approach someone on the street and ask them, "What is your purpose in life?" most would stare at you blankly. They would not have a clue as to how to state their purpose, simply because they have never taken time to put it into words.

If an individual does answer you, they're likely to respond with a goal, not a purpose. These goals may be short term, for example, "to make it through the week" or "to get my taxes done." They might even be broader goals such as "to find a good job," "to stay healthy," or "to travel the world." These are worthy aspirations, but they are not your purpose. Why? Because they're too small.

Remember the saying, "Your purpose in life is to decide what your purpose in life is and to get it done." If that is true, you must find your purpose and put it into words.

Once you decide what your purpose is, your task is to "get it done." In other words, to commit to accomplishing your purpose, remaining conscious of it, never losing sight of it, and continuing to shape your plans and goals around that one over-arching objective.

What is the difference between a life that is purpose-driven and one that is not? The answer: All the difference in the world! Start now by writing out what comes to mind when you read the following unfinished sentence:

MY PURPOSE IN LIFE IS TO _____

_____

_____

_____

Keep thinking about your purpose. It's perfectly all right not to know, as long as you keep *seeking*. And when you know, when you are able to complete the sentence, you will be in a position to help others find their purposes as well.

CHAPTER SUMMARY

This book is preparing you to turn your passion into a coaching business. In order to best apply the business insights discussed later in this book, you will need to have some idea of at least one passion you will use as the foundation of the upcoming exercises and strategies.

This book is intended to give focus, voice, and structure to your passion. Let's recap the five ways I recommend uncovering your passion before moving forward. In this chapter, we covered five indicators that can act like signposts on your way to clarifying your passion:

Number One: Examining what you have already invested in or direct the majority of your resources toward. "Resources" in this situation refers to money, time, and attention.

Number Two: Identifying your natural inclinations. What things are you predisposed to enjoy or dislike?

Number Three: Considering your heart's dream. What things do you find yourself fantasizing about?

Number Four: Your motivations. What factors get you out of bed in the morning?

Number Five: The opportunity to help others and areas where you already give freely of your resources and talents without compensation.

Remember that clarifying your purpose in life and steadily allowing it to guide your goals and actions is essential to your success.

The Lifestyle Millionaire Coaching method offers a way to help others while helping yourself. At this point, you still may not know how to transform your passion into a coaching business but we have begun to chart the territory such that the map indicating how to go from here to where you want is taking shape.

In the next chapters, you will learn how to pursue your passion, the opportunity that Lifestyle Millionaire Coaching offers, and how to coach others on your passion.

CHAPTER TWO

PURSUING YOUR 'REAL' PASSION

I f you are going to coach clients about your passion, it stands to reason that you must learn all you can about the subject. You probably already know a great deal about your topic but that should be only the beginning. Research is in order.

In order to attract and coach others who are interested in your topic, you need to be seen as an accomplished individual, expert, or authority. As a coach, you can (and almost always will) learn from your clients (more about this later). However, you may lose credibility or authority if your clients know more than you do.

In pursuing your passion-based business, the first order of business is to

EXPAND YOUR KNOWLEDGE.

Let's suppose your passion is holistic health. You first need to ask yourself, "How much do I already know about this topic?"

Being truthful in this response is critical because it will guide your next steps and how you spend a great deal of initial time.

Not sure how to answer that question? Here are a few thought-provoking indicators you can use to gain clarity. Add your own topic in the brackets to further personalize this exercise.

- What is meant by the term [insert buzz words from your industry here]?

- What are the top ten reasons people **do/like** [your topic here]?

- What are the top ten reasons people **don't do/dislike** [your topic here]?

- What are the top ten reasons people **start** [your topic here]?

- What are the top ten reasons people **stop** [your topic here]?

- How do most people go about learning [your topic here]? What common training/learning models are being questioned today? To what extent? For what reasons?

- What is the history of [your topic here] in [country name (repeat this question for multiple countries, as it relates to your topic)]?

- What philosophies or worldviews are attached to or stem from [your topic here]?

- How do most people regard [your topic here]?

- What do most people know about [your topic here]?

- What common misconceptions do people have about [your topic here]?

- How are [experts/celebrities in your field] trained?

- How is [your passion] practiced/perceived differently across the world? To what effect?

- What have you learned about the benefits of [your topic] through your own practice? Through others' practice and experience?

- What is happening in the marketing of [insert your topic here]?

As you expand your general study of your passion, you will undoubtedly find yourself drawn to one aspect or another. Returning to our holistic medicine example to put this in context, perhaps you are interested in the products you use and begin to explore how you might market them. On the other hand, you could be most drawn to the psychology of holistic health referred to as the "mind/body/spirit" side. Specifically, you may want to know more about how the mind affects the body to promote its health. This leads you to find yourself particularly fascinated by a Buddhist-based philosophy and practice known as *mindfulness* that is rapidly increasing in popularity throughout the American West Coast.

Remember that research is not limited to reading books. Look for movies, YouTube videos, blogs, seminars, online training, or discussion panels with experts in your area.

What happens if your research draws you down a particular path of interest far away from your formal education or training? For example, through your research you discover that the mindfulness philosophy is making inroads in the business world. That's fascinating to you, but your background is in education.

When this happens, don't shut down or quit! Instead, look for cross-applications. For example, think, "In what ways could mindfulness be applied in schools?" Suddenly you get the idea to train young children in the practice of finding laser-sharp focus. Now you're on to something!

You might continue to explore this application and decide, "This is my passion! I want to train educators how to teach mindfulness to their students." And there you have it!

The second principle of pursuing your passion, then, is to

NARROW DOWN YOUR PASSION.

Once you identify your passion (in this case, holistic health), narrow down your area of interest by searching for what in *particular* you are passionate about within that category. I'll share a personal story from my own life to give you another example.

As a boy in Japan, I wanted to learn English, but going to America without the ability to speak was out of the question. So what did I do? I raced to enroll in basic English courses at a university in Japan.

While taking courses in spoken English, I searched for other resources that could help me. One day the idea hit me: Why not invite an English student to live in our home? Not only would I constantly be around the sounds of the language, but I would also have access to an on-site consultant! I could ask him questions and practice with him for hours.

I followed through with this strategy and the results were excellent. I became an "expert" on the English language precisely because I didn't know English, had a massive need to know it, and was forced to learn it.

Even when I started my English coaching business, I looked back on that year of effectively submersing myself in learning with an expert as one of the most critical steps in my journey..

Thus, the third principle of pursuing your passion is to

USE UNCONVENTIONAL THINKING.

Put yourself in situations where you will be forced to learn more. Keep searching for ways to deepen your knowledge of your subject area. Approach your topic from as many angles as you can. Try reading comments in the discussion section of blogs related to your topic or talk about your passion with a colleague or someone from a different background to hear how they perceive or would approach learning about your passion.

The good news is that "thinking outside the box" is a skill you can develop. Here are some ways to stimulate original thought or come up with creative solutions:

- *Get distance from your routines.* Teach yourself to shave or apply make-up with your other hand. Take a different way to work. If you read romance books all the time, break open a mystery. Do whatever works to get your brain thinking in new ways.

- *Write it out.* Do brainstorming. Take a legal pad and write the issue or problem at the top of a fresh page (for instance, *How to find mindfulness coaching clients who are educators*). Set a timer and commit to writing respons-es to that question, without stopping, for fifteen minutes. During that time, don't hesitate. Don't edit. Don't judge. Just keep writing and see what flows. Quite often, breakthroughs are the result of a diversion from a tributary of an idea that you began halfway through the writing period. In those situations, it's almost as if you found an answer that was hiding in your subconscious, tucked away from all the usual routes your train of thought takes while sorting out problems. If you hadn't forced yourself to keep writing and flesh out all possible options without fear of judgment, you probably never would have come across them.

- *Purposely conceptualize it.* Turn it upside down. Work backwards. If you are thinking broadly, narrow down the problem. If you are concentrating too much, take a step back. Think of this as climbing to the top of a tree to survey the forest for a change.

- *Use positive thinking.* Create an affirmation—a positive statement in the present tense that challenges negativity and makes you smile. For example, "My mind has its own unique way of finding solutions." "People are naturally drawn to me." "Success is looking for me." Post the affirmation where you will come across it (such as on the mirror, refrigerator, or car dashboard). Repeat it often to change your frame of mind.

By now you are beginning to understand that Lifestyle Millionaire Coaching involves introspection, purpose, and action. In this book, you are challenged to take steps to fuel your inner desire and bolster your will to succeed. Without determination, no one would be able to build a successful business.

In the remainder of this chapter I will briefly cover five key areas of personal development (often called "character development") that are the psychological and spiritual foundation blocks for building any sound, reputable business. I am presenting them as your own coach, to provide an example for when you will use them later to coach your clients.

The key areas are

1. Integrity

2. Listening to your own voice

3. Managing self-talk

4. Associations

5. Persistence

Let's look closer at these five key areas of personal development now so you can understand and apply them in your own life.

1. Integrity

What is integrity? It is the ability to act with honesty and to base all your actions on your own moral compass. It is that "special something" found in a person of true self-belief, whose word is their bond. When you have it, integrity will attract clients and inspire them to further grow their own integrity. Since your reputation and relationships are all you really have, integrity is synonymous with trust in the business world.

Integrity is always important, but it is especially so in the Lifestyle Millionaire Coaching model. Why? Because as a Lifestyle Millionaire Coach (LMC) you are not only coaching clients, you are training them to be coaches themselves. This positive feedback

"DO THE RIGHT THING, ESPECIALLY WHEN NO ONE ELSE IS LOOKING."

AKIRA IGUCHI

loop is built into the LMC method and makes integrity fundamental because you set the example for your clients, who then set the example for their clients. Thus, your actions and examples become the template that all future followers base themselves on.

That's why your belief in yourself is the foundation on which you will successfully build your Lifestyle Millionaire Coaching business.

2. Listening to Your Own Voice

Finding and learning to listen to your own voice is a very important concept in achieving success. What does that look like in practice? I can best illustrate it by again pulling from my own experience.

Looking back, I knew no one was going to show up and lead me on the path I needed to travel. I had only myself to answer to. And so there came a turning point when I suddenly realized I needed to follow my self, ideas, and advice.

At my low, I'd barely graduated from high school, had a severe lack of self-confidence, and was clinging to a mind-set that shouted, "Life is hard!" I was so afraid of social rejection and bullying that I began to fear being around people in general. I was alone, always—if not physically then emotionally.

At that point, I looked inside of myself and realized I had only two things and I knew just one thing. I had hope and a vague belief that I could do more. I knew I had to do something.

So I went down to the Hotel Hankyu International in Osaka and got a job as a waiter in the bar. I only made $7.00 an hour and tips but it was a start. The physical aspect of the job and rules of etiquette were grueling to me but I stuck with it for one thing: the social scene.

After work, all the staffers would talk, laugh, and hang out over drinks. As I joined them day after day, I began to feel a sensation I had nearly forgotten: belonging. I started to see that I could have a place in society and maybe this was where I could have a career, too.

After about eighteen months, my coworkers started asking me what I would do next. I confidently replied, "Maybe I will work here full time!"

Their faces fell. "But you're not going to be paid well. And the hours are terrible. And the work is hard," they complained.

I paused and reflected on how many blisters I had from running drinks around the massive bar for hours on end every day. I replayed my memories of all the times I'd accidentally dropped a drink and my furious manager told me each drink was equal to an hour's income.

Then I traced the outlines of all the patrons in the bar enjoying drinks that cost me an entire hour to afford. I heard the soundtrack of their laughter and admired their joyful, carefree gestures.

My colleague's reply hit me like a ton of bricks.

The next day, with no plan in my head but a fire in my soul, I walked up to the infamous furious manager and quit.

I walked out of the bar and aimlessly into the bustling streets of Osaka. My decision hadn't yet set in but I somehow had a vague feeling that my next step was right around the corner.

On that corner, in fact, was a bookstore. Tony Robbins' Unlimited Power lured me off the street and inside. Having hated school and no exposure to business, the business section of a bookstore was as familiar to me as a desert island. I picked up Robbins' book. It was fifteen dollars—two hours of work at the bar job I now no longer had—but something inside told me to buy it.

I handed over the cash, rushed home and started to read it right away. Within the pages of that little book, I started to learn things that no one had ever taught me. Those chapters became the starting point for some of the greatest chapters of my life.

The phrase "with no plan in place but a fire inside" captures exactly how I felt that day in Osaka. I was cutting a cord, burning a bridge, saying goodbye.

Think about your own life now. Think about the times when you realized you needed to listen to yourself, to your own voice. Was it when you were faced with a hard decision and others were telling you what to do but something inside was leading you in another direction? How did it turn out?

At that point in my life, even though I didn't fully realize my passion, my instincts were speaking to me. I was using resources that fell in my path, like the business book, to point myself in an unknown direction.

Someday you, too, will have to go forward into the unknown without a compass, trusting only your intuition. You will find, too, that once you let go and follow your own path, what looked like walls before can suddenly become opening doors. Why not start now?

The day I bought Unlimited Power, I had already veered off the normal life path—go to school, study hard, go to college, get a good job, work for forty years, and retire. Since nearly everyone I knew then was on that path, I assumed (or sometimes they'd remind me) that I'd never be successful.

But within the pages of Unlimited Power I learned that there are other ways to be successful while being just who you are. I discov-

ered something I'd never known before—that you can do anything you want. And better yet? You can do it through positive thinking, goal setting, and marketing.

Somehow I knew I could do these things but I still didn't know how.

As I read and studied the book, I realized that all the examples were about people in America. At that, I decided to leave Japan and move to the U.S.A. After all, I wasn't happy in Japan. I didn't fit in. I didn't have a job, wife, or house to tie me down.

So it was decided—I would start a new life in the U.S. There was only one small problem: I didn't speak a word of English.

Before the end of the night, I raced to enroll in English courses at the nearest university. Along with my two daily classes, I listened to English CDs every day. Some classmates spoke English so well that I was shocked. I thought to myself, if they can do it I could, too! My growing English abilities started to change my life. And for the possibly the first time ever, I was inspired.

What have you noticed about this phase of my life? Many people could conclude that not knowing how to speak English was a tremendous barrier to my progress and achieving my dream. By using it as an enabler of my progress instead of an obstacle, I was able to turn it into an advantage. Learning English was to become the basis of my future business!

So here is a secret: once you take the step to trust yourself and leave the old society-supplied assumptions about life and success behind, you might find that even the most discouraging events and circumstances are there to point you to where you're supposed to go.

As a Lifestyle Millionaire Coach, listening to your own voice must become a habit. When you sharpen your "inner hearing" and learn to recognize the signals intuitively, you will gradually become an inner-directed person whose destiny rests in their own hands, not the criticisms of other people or the prevailing winds of society.

3. Managing Self-Talk

I've been telling you about the importance of believing in yourself. But do you know that believing is a *practice?* The truth is, you believe in yourself only to the extent that you've made a *practice* of doing so.

Our beliefs, including those about ourselves, are malleable. Once you recognize this, you can go about rooting out negative beliefs and attitudes—the inner whispers that bring you down or hold you back, tell you that you can't, won't, or it's useless to do something. You can then change your beliefs to be more in line with the success you are seeking.

The most important reason to purposely change your self-restricting ideas is because your beliefs drive your behavior. They act as filters for your perceptions. You see only what fits your beliefs and ignore what doesn't. This means you could be feeling just as good about yourself as you feel bad about yourself. Who is to say which is right? Only you.

The Power of Affirmation

When you help your client identify a limiting belief (for example, *"I can't seem to make money"* . . . *"I'm not good with people"* . . . *"I don't have the business gene"* . . . *"I don't manage time well"* . . . *"People aren't attracted to me"*), remember that they have been practicing that limiting belief for a while. In order to start feeling differently toward themselves, they must embark on a mission of changing their beliefs. In order to challenge it, you will need to help them construct and practice a new belief.

The best way to change a belief is through the use of *affirmations*. An affirmation is a declaration of new truth you want to create. Let's look at some examples of affirmations now, to bring more clarity to this topic.

Tell your client: If the little voice in your head beats you up with a message like:

- I am stupid . . . *Tell yourself* . . .

  I have a uniquely functioning mind.

- I am clumsy . . . *Tell yourself* . . .

  I float like a butterfly.

- No one likes me . . . *Tell yourself* . . .

  People secretly admire me.

- I don't belong. . . . *Tell yourself* . . .

  I have a special place in this world.

- I can't get ahead. . . . *Tell yourself* . . .

  Good things are looking for me.

Look at the list of affirmations above (the column on the right). Notice that they: (a) are expressed in the present tense; (b) have no negatives (no "nots"); (c) are playful and outrageous, as if designed to shock the sensibility into a new game.

Even though you should take your new affirmation seriously, it should make you smile whenever you think of it or see it posted.

Take out a piece of paper now and write an affirmation that will fly in the face of the previous Killer Statement. It may take several tries. Keep playing around with it until you come up with just the right wording. It should follow these guidelines:

- It is positive.

- It is in the present tense.

- It uses metaphors.

- It makes you smile and lightens your mood.

Affirmation

As you and your client create affirmations and practice repeating them daily, be aware that your mind will be resistant to giving up its old familiar put-downs. It might scoff at the new saying, saying it's just a joke or wishful thinking. That's where controlling your mind comes into play. Train yourself to think in this new way by writing the affirmation down and posting it wherever you'll come across it—on the fridge, bathroom mirror, or car dashboard.

Better yet, share it with somebody in an email or live discussion. Remember, you are helping yourself and your client train new belief muscles in the mind, so *practice* is what will make the difference.

COACHING MODEL: The Power of Reframing

To reframe is to see something differently without changing the facts. Look at the picture below. Perhaps at first you see a skull. But what else do you see? If you can discern a beautiful woman looking in a boudoir mirror, you have reframed the picture.

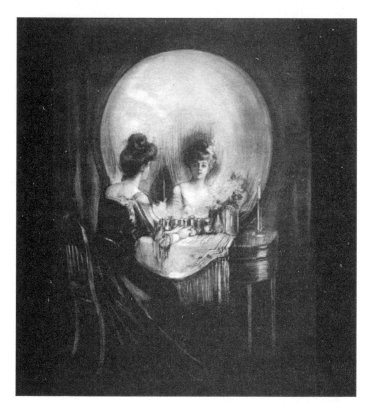

Now, notice that each way you see the picture carries with it a different emotional tone. When you reframe something, whether it's a job, relationship, illness, or problem, you change not only the way you see it but how you feel about it.

Think now about how you can use this reframing technique on your passion and on the business you want to create from it.

Think also about how you can help your coaching clients by teaching them to reframe a situation.

You might ask such questions as

- How can you look at this situation differently?

- Are you able to step back and view this problem in a new light?

- Can you let go of the way you are seeing this and just be open to what comes?

- What's between you and changing the way you look at this?

- What's the payoff (even a negative one) for continuing to see this the way that you currently do?

When you looked at the skull and lady picture above, your mind had to let go of seeing it one way in order to see it the other way. Thus, to help yourself or your client (who may be stuck in a myopic mind-set) reframe, you'll probably need to help them focus on letting go of the "skull" before they can see the "lady." Thus, they may have to reframe their circumstances from discouraging to hopeful, from options-less to options-full, from being a victim to being in charge, in order to create their breakthrough.

"NO MATTER WHAT'S HAPPENING, YOU CAN ALWAYS REFRAME IT."

AKIRA IGUCHI

4. Persisting

Sometimes, just when you think you're on the train to success and nothing can interrupt your ride, you enter a dark tunnel where not only does all that elation and excitement fade away, but you also lose your sense of purpose and confidence in yourself.

I was not in Buffalo anymore. It was difficult, intense. This college seemed packed to the brim with students who never slept in the city that never sleeps. Constantly rushing from one place to another, the other students were hard to interact and make friends with. It didn't help that I was still intensely shy at the time and terrified of talking to strangers. The dark, somber feelings of isolation started to creep back in. It felt like returning to my high school years.

Suddenly, my vision and purpose became blurred. I didn't sleep well or eat healthy. I started slipping into depression and a downward spiral began to envelop my life as things unraveled. I got homesick and I started skipping school. When I looked in the mirror, all I saw was a failure, again.

One day, in a moment of true homesickness and despair, I called my mom from a pay phone on the street. Taxis and trucks whizzed past throngs of people bustling on without notice. It was bitter cold and dark. I stood shivering at the phone as I told my mom, "It's so tough, so hard here." I detailed all the ways that life in the city was worse than life back in Buffalo, New York.

At the end of the call my mom said, "I've never lived outside of Japan, so I don't know what to say."

I hadn't asked her anything. I couldn't seem to speak the words my heart was screaming, "Please help!"

As I looked out into the dark, chilly night, I remembered how much time, effort, and sacrifice I'd made to get to this very street. I couldn't just give up and go back. But at the same time, I felt too powerless to go forward. I was stuck, miserable, depressed.

For the next four months, I endured that same cold, piercing darkness.

By the end of the semester, I couldn't even go to school. All I could think was, "How can I get out of my life?"

Each day had become so dark, isolated, and hopeless I considered leaving them behind, ending it.

Yet the question didn't go away, "How do I get out of this life?"

Upon reflection, it's clear to me that losing my sense of purpose was the trigger that made me feel lost in every other aspect of my life. But even though I'd lost sight of my purpose, as you will see, my purpose hadn't lost sight of me. I had yet to realize that being on purpose often means discovering that you're already on it.

All of us have low points, times when we feel stopped or confused and disoriented. Especially in times of perceived failure, hope can seem to vanish and things begin to look bleak.

Few of us actively seek low times, yet upon looking back, we often recognize that many of our greatest breakthroughs occurred when things seemed most hopeless. Failures turned out to be opportunities and setbacks actually opened doors.

It was December in New York and the silent falling snow cast a hush upon the city. I sat in my tiny studio and looked out the window. I lived on the fourth floor and the view was awful—garbage and dirty snow piles were nearly all I could see. In my depressed state, everything seemed ugly and wrong.

It was from that view that I reasoned, "If I jump from here, I would be able to get out of this life."

A few thoughts later, my life changed.

As I stood there at the window drowning in my own desperation to escape my life, a song came over my radio: "Hero" by Mariah Carey.

The words filled my tiny apartment. "There is a hero if you look inside your heart."

The song rushed over me, seeming to speak directly to my heart. I stood in the window watching the snow and let Mariah's words overpower the whispers in my head.

HERO
BY MARIAH CAREY

There's a hero

If you look inside your heart

You don't have to be afraid

of what you are

There's an answer

if you reach into your soul

And the sorrow that you know

will melt away

And then a hero comes along

With the strength to carry on

And you cast your fears aside

And you know you can survive

So when you feel like hope is gone

Look inside you and be strong

And you'll finally see the truth

That a hero lies in you

It's a long, road

When you face the world alone

No one reaches out a hand

For you to hold

You can find love

If you search within yourself

And the emptiness you felt

Will disappear

And then a hero comes along

With the strength to carry on

And you cast your fears aside

And you know you can survive

So when you feel like hope is gone

Look inside

And then a hero comes along

With the strength to carry on

And you cast your fears aside

And you know you can survive

So when you feel like hope is gone

Look inside you and be strong

And you'll finally see the truth

That a hero lies in you

I got goose bumps all over. I thought, "Wow, that's true." I didn't just think the song was true. I knew it was true.

Sometimes the moments that change everything occur when you least expect them. And oftentimes it is from the depth of our own wintery despair that we discover our own invincible spring.

The song was right—I had been looking for the answer outside of myself: in society, in my teachers, in my parents, in culture, in other voices. I'd never listened to my voice.

I decided right there, right then, standing and watching the snow from my window, to listen to my own voice. I was crying. It was traumatic. But it was also a turning point in my difficult world.

I committed to finding the hero inside of myself.

After that night, I started doing what I hadn't before. I started talking to strangers, interacting with my classmates, and making friends.

Suddenly, I knew how to think positively. I began attending personal development seminars. The first time I went to a live seminar, the power and inspiration of the event shocked me. I thought to myself, "Wow, this is so powerful! I'm ready for this!" Little by little, I took baby steps and realized I could change.

My very first seminar was hosted by the author of the book that inspired my interest in English and my dream to move to America—Tony Robbins himself. In just that short period of seminar time, I saw people transform their lives. I was mesmerized.

Tony's message hit me in right in the heart. Even though I'd read some of his content already, his speeches convinced me that anything was possible. I realized that I could do, be, and have anything I wanted. I held the power to transform my life.

As I listened to Tony speak on "Unleashing the Power Within," I realized that I, too, had power within me. He spoke about how deep emotion isn't always a bad thing. In fact, that deep emotion can hold the secret to unlocking your passion and motivation. Just like my emotions that night at the window had reignited my desire to survive, succeed, and pursue my dreams, as I listened to Tony, I realized that I wanted to be like him.

That day change my perspective. I suddenly knew I wanted to help people. I wanted to inspire others. And this time, my potential felt unlimited.

COACHING CAN CHANGE LIVES

That seminar gave me an incredibly powerful gift as a young man sitting in the audience. Have you had a similar experience? Did you receive it as a thunderbolt, like I did? Or did it come slowly, as the truth dawned upon you that you were in charge of yourself, that you had only yourself to answer to for how your life was going to turn out?

What words made the difference in your life? Whose encouragement and guidance has had the most impact on you? In whose company did you first hear your own voice? Was it a parent or grandparent? A teacher or coach? A boss or co-worker? A friend?

Research on resilience in children has shown conclusively that a single factor makes the difference between whether or not kids from drug- and crime-ridden upbringings will have productive, healthy lives. That factor is: *a relationship with a caring adult.*

That's right, the presence of a mentor, guide, or role model determines the difference between kids from tough backgrounds becoming valuable, contributing members of society and spiraling down into the same drug- or crime-filled lives as they were raised in.

As a coach, you stand to make that kind of difference in the lives of your clients. Through your work as a Lifestyle Millionaire Coach, you can repeatedly experience the deep satisfaction that comes from bringing real benefit to others. You might even enable others to find their voice, passion, or purpose.

Recall my personal story of desperation on a New York City window ledge in winter. The life-changing impact of words (like Mariah Carey's, in my life) can change not only you but also your clients as you skillfully coach them to listen to their own aspirations and values, especially when they are countercultural. The coaching skills you will develop as an LMC can enable you to experience that sublime fulfillment again and again.

KEEPING PERSPECTIVE

At this point in the book, a certain warning is in order. While I have been coaching and encouraging you to develop and practice these positive traits, be aware that not everyone will be open to doing the same.

We tend to project our own values and positive aspects onto others. So you must be careful not to expect everyone to live up to your values. And when you meet people who are untrusting, they will be cautious and treat you as if you are untrustworthy. Don't be surprised if it takes them a while to trust you.

The story of my early life is a rather dramatic one. I took risks and made decisions that may have you thinking: "Wait a minute. Are you expecting me to do that, too? I've got a job. Other people are depending on me. I can't afford just to just drop everything and start a new business from scratch."

Rest assured, no one expects you to do such things. For nearly everyone, becoming a Lifestyle Millionaire Coach is a "side business," something you begin slowly and develop over weekends or in your spare time. Gradually, it will build and begin to produce results on its own, aside from your present work.

In the next chapter, we will explore this in more detail.

CHAPTER SUMMARY

Through sharing the story of my own personal journey, I have attempted to illustrate some key qualities and values that have made an incredible difference in my life. I highly recommend you develop these same traits on your way to building a Lifestyle Millionaire Coaching business.

This chapter has recommended ways that you can work on yourself to prepare an in-depth knowledge of your passion. Three key strategies—expanding your knowledge, finding your specialty or niche, and using unconventional thinking—will help you to deepen your expertise in your field.

I invite you to apply these key principles to your own thinking and experience. Then, use these same values to coach your clients—not by preaching about them or even necessarily mentioning them but through the underlying support, understanding, and encouragement you convey as you guide them through their challenges and difficulties in starting their own Lifestyle Millionaire Coaching journeys.

Let's recap these values now for enhanced recollection:

Number One: integrity.

Number Two: listening to your own voice.

Number Three: managing self-talk.

Number Four: good associations.

Number Five: persistence.

A final note on the importance of persistence and dedication to your passion and Lifestyle Millionaire Coaching business: Like me, at times you might become lost and discouraged, wanting to give it all up. Often, it's at this darkest hour that a light shines through and restores your belief that everything is going to be all right. But even without that, you need to endure to realize your passion and watch it come to fruition. Reframing is also a powerful skill to use and to coach others to use.

To close this chapter, I will share a powerful excerpt entitled *Paradoxical Commandments* written by Kent M. Keith, an American writer and leader in higher education. I believe this excerpt embodies what this chapter and Lifestyle Millionaire Coaching itself is all about: trusting your own sense of what is right and acting on it.

Paradoxical Commandments of Leadership

1. People are illogical, unreasonable and self-centered.

   Love them anyway.

2. If you do good, people will accuse you of selfish ulterior motives.

   Do good anyway.

3. If you are successful, you win false friends and true enemies.

   Succeed anyway.

4. The good you do today will be forgotten tomorrow.

   Do good anyway.

5. Honesty and frankness make you vulnerable.

   Be honest and frank anyway.

6. The biggest people with the biggest ideas can be shot down by the smallest people with the smallest minds.

   Think big anyway.

7. People favor underdogs but follow only top dogs.

   Fight for a few underdogs anyway.

8. What you spend years building may be destroyed overnight.

   Build anyway.

9. People really need help, but may attack you if you do help them.

   Help them anyway.

10. Give the world the best you have and you'll get kicked in the teeth.

    Give the world the best you have anyway.

CHAPTER THREE
YOUR BIGGEST OPPORTUNITY

I f you are looking for an opportunity to be rewarded with results and make a difference in the lives of others, Lifestyle Millionaire Coaching is ideal for you. These two motivations—to succeed and to help others to succeed—will fuel your efforts in the new career that is waiting for you.

In this chapter, we will consider the vast opportunities that await individuals who seek to coach others in their area of passion-related expertise. When we look at how coaching began and where it is now, it becomes clear that your chances for success are multiplying.

At twenty-years-old, I didn't speak English well but I was passionate about learning to do so—and quickly. Fortunately, I spoke enough of the language to attend university in the United States. I took courses, read books, and was privileged to have a wonderful mentor, a college professor, who recognized my deep motivation and took me under her wing. From her I learned more than English. I learned to think about the American culture around me.

I had a teacher but not a coach, so I invented my own. I was excited, ready to learn, and asked myself the important questions a coach would ask:

- *Why do you want to do this?*
- *What are the deeper reasons that connect your desire to who you really are?*
- *Where do you want to go with this?*
- *What are you willing to sacrifice in order to get there?*

Although I could not know it at the time, this kind of inner exploration would lead me to the nature of coaching, the role that would build my career.

A BRIEF HISTORY OF COACHING

What is a coach? A coach is a person who supports a learner in achieving a specific personal or professional goal. Coaching has a number of theoretical origins including sports psychology, the human potential movement, and business management. Coaching began in the sports world but its growth as an industry has undergone many changes.

In the first half of the twentieth century, Dale Carnegie tapped into people's desire for self-improvement with his book *How to Win Friends and Influence People.* He also developed training courses on sales and business leadership.

Three decades later, in 1968, Og Mandino wrote the best-selling book *The Greatest Salesman in the World,* followed by other inspirational books promoting a successful and happy life.

More recently, several key figures contributed to the transformation of coaching into the industry it is today. The most noteworthy individuals in this category include Timothy Galway (author of *The Inner Game of Tennis*), Werner Erhard (founder of EST training), and Thomas Leonard, who synthesized the strains of financial management, achievement, and personal growth into "life coaching" and made it a popular concept.

Corporate formal business training became standard in the 1960s. But managers quickly realized that often people who go through training in some skill or concept tend to forget what they learned and revert to previous habits. Coaching helped consolidate and solidify learning from training, enabling the effects and outcomes to become ongoing.

Another aspect of business—high turnover—necessitated an explosion of coaching. Whereas people used to stay in one job for a lifetime, they now change careers an average of three times.

The period from 1990 to 2004 saw coaching emerge as a distinct profession. Combined with a growing interest in human potential, this led to a tipping point in coaching, the moment of critical mass or boiling point where the idea suddenly caught on and spread broadly.

TURBULENCE—
AN EXTRAORDINARY OPPORTUNITY

What makes the present—this particular period from 2013 to 2020—so favorable for someone entering the coaching profession? The answer is simple: *turmoil*. Not only is change taking place on all levels at a mind-boggling pace, people must deal with the *ongoing acceleration* of that change. Each year, each quarter, and each month, the dial creeps up. More demands, more to handle, more to confuse. And amid it all, people feel a vast sense of unpredictability and disorder.

I call this predicament a silent earthquake. People are waking up each morning with an intangible sense of worry and tension. They know the day is not likely to go as planned. They must shift gears, think on their feet, and dance on the rugs as they are pulled out from underneath them. We are being asked to learn to live in a new way in a new world with its proliferation of inputs and stimuli clamoring for attention. Could you imagine a more perfect environment for support and an understanding ear?

With mass dependence on the Internet, cell phones, and other products of the rapid technological explosion, coaching helps people deal with the stress and time pressures of turbulent times.

Here's another way to look at the role of a coach in today's world: imagine that you are an expert white-water kayaker helping others learn to overcome rapids, maneuver over falls, avoid rocks, and successfully keep their small crafts above water and on track.

This metaphor is closer to the truth than you think. You may not actually be a world-class paddler but your own growth and life experiences more than qualify you to help your fellow citizens through the fearful turbulence of change.

Although people say they are looking for financial success, finances are often just a small part of the problem. What they are really craving is advice about their lives in general.

That insight is so powerful, I will write it again: Although people say they want financial success, they're often actually craving advice about how to live their lives, in general.

The position of life coach is more needed and in demand today than ever. Why? Because *a life coach is someone who aims to help and empower others to make, meet and exceed personal and professional goals—including excelling in the workplace, becoming happy and fulfilled in the home, exploring the self and the world, and achieving ambitions.*

THE ROLE OF TECHNOLOGY

Back, you know, a few generations ago, people didn't have a wayto share information and express their opinions efficiently to a lot of people. But now they do. Right now, with social networks and other tools on the Internet, all of these 500 million people have a way to say what they're thinking and have their voice be heard.

—Mark Zuckerberg, founder of Facebook

In thinking about the proliferation of current means by which you are able to market yourself, attract clients, and coach them, consider this: Even when the coaching industry was booming in the early nineties, *there was no Internet. There were no cell phones. No social media. No Skype.*

Today it is vastly different. Millions of people are online every hour of every day, using their cell phones, tablets, and other handheld devices. There has never been a greater variety of tools for reaching out to people in need.

Ironically, there is even a massive opportunity to use technology to help people who are overwhelmed and stressed because of the role and challenges created by technology in their lives.

NATIONS OF OPPORTUNITY

Remember when it was socially acceptable to say things like, "I don't do any of that 'computer' stuff"? Today, support for that opinion is disappearing fast, not only in American but also around the world.

The world is online and that means that the scope of your coaching opportunity is not limited to one country. All English-speaking areas of the world have people who can relate in some way to your passion and who are thus open to your influence.

One way to think about this is to mentally divide the world not into geographical areas but into "nations of passion." To understand what this means, let us return to the example of the mindfulness curriculum.

In that example, the hypothetical you was drawn to the field of holistic health. Within that field, your interest narrowed to combine with your interest in childhood education. Finally, you identified your passion—the area of *mindfulness education.*

To apply the metaphor of "nations" of passion to this example, we will think about the Nation of Holistic Health, made up of all the people who share your interest in this area. Within that nation are subdivisions or "states" representing more specialized interests. You will find your fellow citizens (who are, remember, spread throughout the world) in the State of Mindfulness (the same way we might say, "in the State of California").

At the same time there is another nation of passion, the Nation of Education. Within that nation there are, let's say, the different states of Early Childhood, Lower Grades, High School, and College. Now consider how these broad nations of Holistic Health and Education (encompassing millions of people) and their subsection "states" might overlap.

Your fellow citizens in the Nation of Lower Grade Education will overlap with those in the State of Mindfulness. The diagram above will help to depict these theoretically, but marketable "nations" and their "states" are a real concept.

The shaded area shows the overlap of the State of Lower Grades Education and the State of Mind-Body Interest—a "city" called Lower Grades Mind-Body (LGMB) made up of people whose passions are *both* lower-grades education and mindfulness. These citizens represent your coaching market. You have narrowed the scope of your own interest, and those of your prospective clients, down to this "city" populated by individuals who, like yourself, want to know more about and work in the area of LGMB.

Remember, in reality, the "citizens" of this Mindfulness Education are spread throughout all the countries of the world and they are accessible through the Internet, social media, Skype, and basically every other electronic means of interaction. Realize also that once your coaching business is up and running, its energy will automatically attract not only these LGMB citizens but also people who have not yet been attracted to this city but are drawn in through online outreach.

The following are comments you can imagine from three persons who are responding to the marketing of your hypothetical business:

1. From a *beginner*, a person who has never had more than a passing thought about your topic: "A teacher who knows of my interest in the social-emotional growth of children told me to look up this blog. After reading the first post, I was hooked!"

2. From a *hobbyist*: "I've found someone who can coach me in my area of interest and I'm excited about all I will learn about this subject!"

3. From a *committed person* who already shares your passion: "This is amazing. Now, I can not only expand my expertise in this area of intense interest to me, I can also be trained to do something I've never thought of—start my own business coaching others!"

BUILDING RIGHT ASSOCIATIONS

Have you noticed that when you keep company with people who enrich you and make you feel good about yourself, you are internally invigorated and your best traits naturally come to the fore? And have you also found that interacting with the wrong kind of people (the pessimists, the cynics, the know-it-alls, the drainers who never add to your world but always subtract from it) brings you down to their level, resulting in self-doubt and discouragement?

It is not so much what is said or done when you are with any of those groups, *just being in that environment is enough for the effects to rub off one you.* This truth, which one could call the Law of Association, works despite our efforts to deny it. So watch out: you are whom you hang out with.

I threw myself into learning English. I made friends with the American professors and hung out with them in their offices. I studied four or five hours every day. Once I felt a certain level of comfort, I wanted more.

My hunger to learn faster even drove me to submit an application to be a host family for an American exchange student without my parents knowing. To my fortune, I got selected! In that year of hosting, I went from speaking not a word to speaking very good English. I became known for my fluency and ability to quickly master the language.

After about a year of studying English, I decided it was time to leave Japan. I set out for America and when I arrived in Buffalo, New York, I was in shock. The days were bitter cold and the snow was seemingly endless. But those were just the details of the town. There was another kind of shock I experienced. This time, it was good.

There were fewer rules in New York than Japan and everyone I met spoke their mind freely and with passion. I was witnessing American individualism firsthand. And the experience thrilled me.

In those overpiled snow banks and negative temperatures, I finally found people like myself.

Whoever you hang out with can either hold you back or push you ahead. That's why it is crucial to evaluate the friends and associates you interact with on a regular basis. While there are situations like work or teams where you can't actually determine with whom to spend your time, you can limit the extra time you spend around them or how deeply you engage with them. You don't have to be negatively judgmental or act better than them, just look around and ask, who inspires and encourages me? Then spend more time with them and slowly decrease your time and exposure to those not in that category.

You might be thinking, "But my good examples are far away" or "I've lost touch with them." In that case, pick up the phone, send an email, or post on their wall. Never underestimate the power of spending time with people you want to be like or friends who see the best that is in you and encourage you. Hours—even moments—spent with such people are like water in the well of your future.

The Law of Association brought me into the lives of so many friends and professors who thought the same way I did. Our interactions often felt like magic! Everything in that new environment spoke to me, telling me that I was right, I was on my way.

So, far away from my house in Osaka, my parents and everything I had ever known, I suddenly felt at home. Better yet—I fit in! An overwhelming sense of relief came with that acceptance because it showed that I wasn't the problem; my environment just wasn't right. I had to go to a completely foreign culture to finally feel at home.

Now, this is not to say I was living like a luxurious Lifestyle Millionaire. I didn't have a cell phone. I lived in a dorm barely larger than my kitchen in Japan yet had to also share it with a roommate. It was my first time living outside of my parent's house and fending for myself.

At the end of one year, my time as an exchange student in Buffalo had run out. But I craved to stay in the U.S. longer. I wanted to more deeply understand the culture. I was reading books about personal and business development during any moment of free time I could find. I wanted to start a business, to become an entrepreneur like the people in that book I'd discovered in the Osaka bookstore.

I decided to go try my luck in the Big Apple for more opportunity. So when my year in Buffalo came to a close, I took a leap of faith and moved to New York City.

"IF OPPORTUNITY DOESN'T KNOCK, BUILD A DOOR."

MILTON BERLE

The Speaking Opportunity

The human voice is the organ of the soul.
—Henry Wadsworth Longfellow

Air is a bearer of knowledge. The human voice has great power. It is a big part of nonverbal bonds we form with people. The voice, after all, comes from deep sources. It is finely tuned by the emotions and conveys the slightest change of feeling. It broadcasts the intention of a speaker and can load the simplest words with complicated meanings.

The human voice has the power to move listeners much more by its rhythm, pattern, and intonation than through the meanings of the words it pronounces. We tend to think of communication as words, but it is the voice that gives the intended meaning to the words.

People don't keep silent about their passions. Instead, they talk about them whenever the opportunity arises. Go to a convention and listen to the noise of the excited crowd during the intermissions. Many came to talk, perhaps more than to listen.

You have been speaking with others—in person, online, by phone, or in writing—perhaps for years, about your passion. Consider the critical part your voice will play in your new coaching business as well. It will be the main vehicle of communication when coaching clients and also how people learn about your services.

Recall my story about the transformational Tony Robbins seminar I attended. All I could think of as I listened to Tony was: *I want to do what he is doing! I can and I will!* It was such a motivating experience that it kick-started my thinking and actions toward formulating my own business.

Think back to a time when a speaker moved you. Do you remember the excitement, the tension, the I-can't-wait-for-what-comes-next feeling? Now imagine that you are the one standing before an audience, presenting a talk or seminar on your passion. Your voice carries excitement and your audience feels it. As your passion grows, you are letting others see into your mind. The audience leans forward in their seats, their eyes sparkling. They can't wait to hear what you have to say!

As you present the key points about starting a coaching business around the topic that has brought you and your audience together, you notice people nodding, smiling, and taking notes. After closing your talk, many of them come forward to meet with you. You have generated enthusiasm through the power of your voice!

Most popular speakers will probably say they got their start by giving a talk to four or five associates in a friend's living room. That is a good way to start. Once you begin, though, the opportunities to grow your business through speaking engagements are prolific. All sorts of organizations—clubs, companies, churches, libraries, conventions, societies, and associations, just to name a few—are constantly looking for speakers who will inform, entertain, and draw audiences. You can find these groups by a simple online search for words and phrases related either to your coaching passion directly or to the kinds of organizations that could bring your audiences together.

Another means of marketing yourself as a speaker are national, state, and local speakers' bureaus. These are organizations dedicated to marketing speakers to events such as conventions, company retreats, and societal meetings. Once you are seen as a person who can attract and hold listeners' interest, you can find yourself invited to speaking engagements without even trying. Of course, these marketing companies will want their share of the payment but that can be worthwhile to you as you make a name for yourself and start out.

Webinars

There is no real substitute for the "live" experience of being in person with a speaker and other audience members. However, speaking live through online channels is a close substitute that can multiply your audience exponentially.

The most popular vehicle for using your voice, speaking ability, and presence to promote your coaching product and reach vast numbers of people at once is a web-based seminar, known as a webinar. Although webinars can be costly, the opportunity to create and host your own webinars is at your fingertips. In fact, with just a YouTube account, you could host a low-budget webinar using Google+ Hangouts.

The Social Media Opportunity

Social media is online content created by people using highly accessible publishing technologies. This form of media has become extremely popular because it allows people to form relationships for personal, political, and business use online. This technology represents a shift in how people discover, read, and share news, information, and content.

Social media has proliferated during the past decade to become a mainstay of life for most people. A 2011 social networking survey found that 65% of U.S. online adults are using a social networking tool like Facebook, LinkedIn, or Twitter. The average American worker is currently spending 1.2 hours daily on social media-related tasks. At present, 61% of online Americans under thirty use social media–related websites on a daily basis. Social media represents a tremendous opportunity for you to build your Lifestyle Millionaire

Coaching business. Your use of social media transforms you into an author.

The Writing Opportunity

When I shared my personal story and reflections on finding your voice earlier in this book, I was referring to an inner matter, a means of instilling trust and confidence in yourself in order to make your own way. Just now I have been talking about your speaking voice as an expression of that inner self. And writing is, of course, another natural and powerful way to communicate your voice and your message to others.

You will continuously rely on writing in your business—for emails, letters, ads, promotions, some magazine or journal articles, and even books. You don't have to be a professional writer or author to express yourself through writing. In fact, the more simple and direct your writing is, the more powerful it can be. People are looking for sincerity in what they read. They want to be informed. They want to be entertained. They want to be inspired. If you focus on those aspects, you can make a large impact with your writing.

The Website Opportunity

One obvious form that writing will take in your Lifestyle Millionaire Coaching business is on your website. Creating a website, like creating a webinar, can be expensive. Also as in the latter case, there are means available now that place the creating and managing of an attractive website for your coaching business well within your budget.

Companies such as WebsiteBuilder.com will furnish you with immediate access to tools that can make a site look however and say whatever you want. You can use one of the many templates available or start from scratch. It's easy to add pages and features such as audio interviews or YouTube tracks. And once your website is up, you can engage SEO (search engine optimization) services or attract traffic more organically to your site on your own. Another website feature to consider is one of the most unique ways to share your voice with the world through writing: a blog.

The Blogging Opportunity

What is a blog? A blog is a frequently updated online personal journal or diary. Originally blogs were known primarily as places for people to write about their day-to-day activities. Their mundane, everyday tasks became fodder for journal entries. Somehow these writers gained a following and the hobby of blogging was born. Today people write about far more interesting topics and the formatting and content has become very similar to that of articles or research. Every day millions of people, some of whom have extremely limited technical abilities, write on their blogs.

The Internet is a medium that is unparalleled in its reach. Never before have average people like us been able to reach a global audience with such ease. Bloggers have the opportunity of reaching hundreds or even thousands of people each and every day. What makes blogging so uniquely powerful, so made-to-order for your Lifestyle Millionaire Coaching business, is its subject matter. If you are able to put some of your coaching know-how into your blog posts, your readers will experience the power of your life coaching firsthand. Further, more individuals will want to hire you to coach them one-on-one by phone or on Skype.

A blog is like your own magazine that you are constantly updating. It's a place to share your thoughts and your passions. By adding a blog to your website, you will be able to exponentially share your thoughts, promote yourself, and enhance your coaching business. Blogging is a way to introduce your readers not only to your passion but also to the concept of running their own coaching business. As you write about them both, you are showing them how it's done.

Through your daily updating of your blog you can inform, entertain, and inspire your readers. The more unique and personal you make your blog—and the more variety you introduce—the more followers will be drawn to it. It's easy to make your blog attractive as well. Whatever the subject of a particular post, you can Google appropriate images to include alongside it. You can run a series of posts on a single subject, use different formats (like storytelling, dialogue, poetry, quotations), and even invite guest writers to contribute.

Whatever you do, the trick is to find where the monetization opportunity meets your passion.

CHAPTER SUMMARY

This chapter focused on the great variety of opportunities available to you as a coach. Beginning with some background on coaching's history, citing key leaders and stages in its development, I used the term Inner Game as a catchall phrase for the constantly expanding field of self-evolution and self-improvement. A simple consideration of the times we live in highlights the chances for coaching business success. The extraordinary acceleration of change, brought about largely by the growth of technology, means that more and more people are stressed and overburdened with responsibilities and demands. Thus, more and more of them will need and seek life coaching.

I then introduced you to the concept of Nations of Interest as a metaphorical way of thinking about people everywhere who share your passion and expanding your outreach to a variety of audiences.

The chapter went into detail about a variety of ways to communicate with prospective and current clients, including through public speaking, social media, writing, webinars, website development, and blogging. All represent powerful opportunities to you as a coach.

CHAPTER FOUR

HOW TO TURN YOUR PASSION INTO PROFIT

H ow do you actually go about coaching others in your passion? To begin, you need to determine your passion. I'll share a bit more of my story now to express how my passion was not initially obvious to me.

I spent a year back in Japan, writing my blog and getting some clients for coaching in English. But even though I was excited about making some money, my earnings were not enough to support me. I still lived with my parents and I was hungry to do more. When I considered my situation, I saw that I was unfulfilled. I had learned English and was even teaching some others to speak the language as well.

Learning excited me the most. You will recall how excited I was to read my first business book. I felt the same excitement at Tony Robbins' seminars. It seemed I could not get enough of the things that later turned out to be my own business.

Of course, at the time I had only moments of awareness about this. I was just a young man soaking up everything I could as fast as possible. I was becoming a pioneer in introducing the human potential movement to Japan.

In my earlier summary of the coaching movement, I mentioned Timothy Gallwey's book The Inner Game of Tennis. In addition to providing an impetus to the coaching movement, that book played a huge part in promoting an interest in human potential. I was excited, not only in that movement but also by the fact that a book could be such a powerful force for change. For the second time a book had enflamed my growing passion. For this reason, I will refer to the human progress movement as the Inner Game. Learning the Inner Game, it turns out, was to become my passion.

Look around your neighborhood and office this week. What do you notice about the large number of unfulfilled people there? Often, it's not that they are unhappy. Most are just bored, jaded, uninterested, and unexcited about their situations.

Growing up in Japan, I vividly remember going to school each morning and observing the grim facial expressions of strangers passing by. They looked as if they just wanted to get the day over with, even as it was only beginning.

Living this experience morning after morning spoke to me. I wanted to do something about it. I wanted to help them. But how?

To find the answer, I only had to look at the tools available in the Inner Game: blogging, one-on-one coaching, seminars, and audio programs.

My passion for learning to use these tools came together at just the right time with the growing momentum of the human potential movement in Japan. I saw immediately that I needed a coaching mentor outside of books or myself. I needed to hire a coach!

Luckily, my research and awareness of industry leaders like Tony Robbins gave me an eye for qualifying a gifted, experienced life coach. From her coaching, I learned to coach.

BECOME A COACHING CLIENT YOURSELF

There are many ways to learn how to coach, from books to online courses, seminars to films, and study audio programs to podcasts. But to me it's obvious that the very best way to learn to be a coach is to have *your own coach*. After all, learning to cook online, through books, and in restaurants will never have the same impact as standing beside your mentor as they guide your hand in the kitchen.

There is absolutely no substitute for being coached in your own life. By that, I don't mean once for a couple of hours or over a weekend every year. I mean long-term, weekly coaching.

Every session with your coach delivers a multitude of benefits to you. First, you experience what it's like to be coached. Second, you gain all the benefits of a learning client, and third, you can learn firsthand from an expert. You will experience firsthand what a typical phone session consists of, for example, review of interim progress, discussion of a current issue, and setting a new goal. You will find out how to ask the right questions. You will discover the power of active listening. You might even learn what methods you find ineffective or less productive. You can include all of this knowledge and understanding in your own coaching practice immediately.

GET OUT THERE!

Suddenly the world of growing my business was opening up to me. I became fascinated with each and every aspect—writing, editing, blogging, marketing, etcetera. My days were whirlwinds of participation—attending seminars, conferences, and entrepreneurial meet-ups. Everywhere I went, I learned from and talked to people. Not only did this build my network, it also attracted the participants for my first three-day seminar.

The key to marketing is generating contacts. For this reason, starting a Lifestyle Millionaire Coaching business is not for shy or stay-at-home types.

To start brainstorming and attracting contacts, sit down and make a list of your social environments—the groups of people you interact with through work, shared interests, or social events. These environments may include your job, church, book club, chamber of commerce, exercise groups, choir, or hobby clubs. You may be surprised to realize how many environments you actively participate in.

Next, under each environment, list the people you know personally or by association who are likely candidates for attending your training.

Wherever you go, see each new encounter as an opportunity to talk up your new business. Look in your local newspaper or social media circles for meetings and groups that you could attend or join.

When you show up, don't be shy. Let everyone know you are available to coach, lead a seminar, blog or speak about your subject area.

NETWORKING

The truth is, people actually want to know what you do. Once you start putting yourself out there, every meeting will lead to someone asking about your business. When you answer them, typically, someone will either show personal interest in it or say, "I know someone who is looking for just what you are offering." When that happens, ask how you can help and get contact information.

My vision of people was what started my marketing and maintained it. As I listened, I heard how uninspired people were by their lives. Everywhere I went, they seemed to be concerned with "business as usual."

In my eyes, this was a form of widespread apathy. Other people who noticed this as well seemed to just express regret that so many lives were so devoid of meaning and fulfillment. For me, though, I thought something more could be done and perceived the observation as a representation of opportunity. If folks were looking for value in their daily lives, I wanted to be the one to help them find it!

So in 2008, I started coaching. I hadn't done it before but I knew I could. The reason for my confidence was my deep belief in coaching. I was 100% certain that coaching could help people improve their lives. That conviction carried over into a belief in myself.

I believe desire plays a major part in building a coaching career. You have to want to help people and believe that coaching is the me-

dium to do so. Your belief in the benefits of coaching will carry you along in times of self-doubt.

I took a huge step forward when I invested in a coach for myself. I was hearing and reading about coaching in Japan and asked myself, "How can I get a coach for myself?"

Putting my question out to my network, I learned that a friend knew a guy who was putting on a three-day life seminar of intensive coaching for small groups in Singapore. My friend knew that I had taught English to many people, so he recommended me to serve as an English-to-Japanese translator for the seminar's host. It wouldn't pay much, but it was an opportunity.

Little did I know how big of an opportunity it would become for me!

During my work at the Singapore event, I got to spend time with the seminar leader, Michael. We were talking one-on-one over a meal one day when I told him that I wanted to be a coach.

He smiled at me as he ate his food and said, "You know how to become a great coach? Hire a great coach, like me."

We talked around about the prospect and finally he told me what the cost would be.

I nearly choked on my lunch. The price was many times more than what I was being paid to translate the event, and my savings were low.

Then I realized, "This is the most important investment I can make right now. If it costs me, it means I believe in it."

We agreed on a three-month working relationship and I paid him 90% of all the money I had at the time.

Looking back, without hesitation, I can say that was the best money I ever spent.

Michael told me how to market—for instance, how to offer free coaching to people for a limited time; then when they see the benefit from it, set up a three-month trial period for a fee.

TWO KEY ATTITUDES

The story of my opportunity in Singapore illustrates the need for an investment mind-set.

To achieve your greatest level of success, you have to be willing to put in your all—time, money, effort, dedication, focus, whatever it takes—knowing that in the end it will come back to you a hundredfold. Without such an attitude of measuring the cost and taking action, you will likely never get to where you want to go.

To illustrate this point further, here are two key attitudes for success in starting a Lifestyle Millionaire Coaching business:

1. BELIEF—Belief in the benefits of coaching, the impacts coaching can make, and the belief in yourself as a coach.

2. INVESTMENT—Willingness to invest in the steps that will take you where you want to go. In most situations, the more it costs you, the greater the payoff. Why? Because generally the highest-paid experts are those with the best results, most experience, or greatest abilities to help you get what you want. Further, when you invest in something expensive, you take it seriously and commit to making the most of it.

Another important aspect of meeting my would-be coach Michael lies in what is known in business as the Law of Who You

Know. When you want to look for a coach, start with the contacts you already have and put the word out. Just taking the step to talk to someone about your need will probably start the ball rolling.

There is a famous quote, often attributed to Johann Goethe, German writer, poet and statesman of the mid-1700s, that sums up what I am saying:

Commitment

Until one is committed, there is always the temptation to hesitate and retreat. The way I see it, when it comes to acts of initiative and creation, there is one elementary truth:

The moment one commits, Providence acts, too.

When you commit, a whole stream of events follows from that decision. Favorable unforeseen incidents, meetings and assistance you could have never planned for can suddenly come your way.

Whatever you can do, or dream you can do, begin it. Boldness has genius, power and magic in it. Begin it now.

Acting on coach Michael's advice and suggestions about how to market myself, in 2008 I started offering free promotional talks about coaching to whomever I could. In these two-hour evening talks, I spoke about how coaching worked and why it was important, its deep benefits to help people overcome their challenges and how coaching could take them from where they were to where they wanted to be. Out of these meetings I was able to get people to sign up for a couple of free coaching sessions. From there, some of them wanted to go on into a three-month paid trial coaching with me.

I was amazed at the response. Before long, I was coaching twenty-seven people, each paying $3,000. I was thrilled! I found myself coaching five people a day, two clients in the morning and then three more at night. I repeated this process five days a week and deliver a life seminar on the weekends. I was making the impact and income that convinced me I could do this forever!

I was suddenly seeing my dream come true. I was hooked on having actual clients and seeing myself as a profitable coach.

This went on for many months. However, it didn't take long for the routine to begin to wear on me. I had become a coaching machine! I was feeling the need to move on. Something had to change. At this point the Who You Know Law kicked in again.

In growing my career, I befriended a man, Richard, who was one of the biggest promoters of Inner Game–type events in the world. Richard was putting on a huge three-day life seminar in Singapore and asked if I would help promote the event and sell tickets. Through email and live speaking events, I talked about how this Singapore seminar would change lives and how they would be different at the end of the event.

When I eventually showed up at the event in Singapore, I was blown away. The speaker was so powerful in moving and motivating his audience that follow-on events, books, and recordings were flying off the sales tables in the back of the room. Moreover, the seminar leader had collected hundreds of email addresses through ticket sales that he would later mail to sell more products and build relationships with the attendees. In this way, the seminar made revenue in ticket sales, back-end sales, and even opened doors for future sales. My mind was suddenly open to a whole new host of opportunities.

THINKING BIGGER

What I observed in Singapore showed me how my thinking needed to expand. Suddenly, I saw seminars in a new light. Before, I had been thinking only in terms of the income from what people paid to attend. Now I saw that the event was similar to the old "free razor" marketing campaigns: give people a free razor as a gift then charge a lot for the blades they need in order to use it.

Before I was even seated in my plane at Singapore Airport, I started putting my bigger-thinking plan into action. I started an on-line newsletter, got in touch with a man who had an online newsletter with one hundred thousand readers and paid him $1,000 to promote me through a link to his readers. Nearly overnight, I had five thousand new email addresses. I began sending out coaching emails packed with value to my new list in order to build a relationship with them and enhance my credibility.

After a month, I decided to use the free-razor approach with my newsletter readers. I offered them attendance at a two-day seminar for only $100 dollars.

Soon, I had 160 sign-ups for the event!

Initially, I was thrilled! Then I got nervous. I had to put on a full show for these guests and wow them! I started renting the event hall and hiring a small team of people to help me set up and run the event.

The first day of the event was mediocre. When I told my audience to sign up for a $5,000 follow-on seminar, only two or three people signed up.

T hat was not good. I stayed up late that night with my team, pondering what to do. That meeting was difficult but it proved to be a very critical one for me. When I took the stage on the second day of the seminar, I was a different person. I had changed my attitude and it came through in the way I spoke. I was more forceful, more assertive. I was a leader.

At the end of that session, people came rushing up to me, filled with excitement. Twenty signed up for my follow-on seminar.

Perhaps you can recall a life-changing event like that, where you were in a certain frame of mind and then, perhaps because the stakes were high and risk was involved, you took the plunge and said, "I am going to be different!"

When you did, didn't you notice that others around you changed as well? On Day One of my seminar, I was worried that people wouldn't like me. That fear tainted my worldview such that when I looked out at the audience, all I saw was a group of faces. Consequently, I was ineffective. To use a show business expression, I could have phoned in the talk.

On Day Two, however, I wasn't thinking about money. Instead of a sea of faces, I saw individuals, one by one, looking into their hearts. Suddenly, I remembered how rewarding it is to coach people. I was inspired by the impact I could make in that room and it made me inspiring to others.

"BY CHANGING YOURSELF, YOU CAN SUPPORT CHANGE IN OTHERS."

AKIRA IGUCHI

COACHING MODEL: Project Consciousness

By following my personal story, by now you probably see that I am a "doer" by nature. I don't do much sitting around and that's probably why I'd recommend you shouldn't either. To build a Lifestyle Millionaire Coaching business, you need to develop what I call "project consciousness," or PC for short.

I first discovered PC when I was trying to learn English. The need was so pressing to me that I thought about it all the time. But something else was going on as well. It seemed that wherever I went, I would find references to the English language. I mean, I found them not only on English signs and billboards in Japan, but in my native language as well. The subject came up no matter where I was or what I was doing.

After I'd learned English and started coaching people to learn it, I found PC at work on my new project—coaching. Everything I saw or heard reminded me in some way of my new career as a life coach. After that, whenever I would come to an important place in my learning of the Inner Game, I would typically become obsessed all over again, this time with the new project. After a while I came to expect it. Having a new project meant another visit from my PC friend. It taught me a lot about how the mind works.

When I'm in PC mode, my mind is on the project 24/7—not just when I'm working on it but wherever I go and whatever I do. It's as if I am doing more than thinking—I am seeing the project everywhere.

In some ways, it's almost like being in love. You are connecting everything with it—whether it's things you read or find online, movies you watch, conversations you have with various people—everything links back to that central thought. There's a kind of magic to it: because my mind is so receptive to the project, the world becomes a place that continuously reminds me of it.

If you have not discovered this secret, give yourself a chance to experience the wonder of project consciousness as you think about your coaching business and begin to build it. And in case you are wondering what benefits you can derive from project consciousness, let me assure you that a good case of PC

- points your mind toward new and innovative directions,
- opens the way for unique solutions to problems,
- helps you think outside the box, and
- uncovers new applications and aspects.

CHAPTER SUMMARY

This chapter focused on how to coach, beginning with recognizing the general need people have to upgrade their lives with energy, vitality, and purpose. We discussed how getting a good coach is one of the best ways of learning how to coach and the two key attitudes necessary for keeping your own enthusiasm high: belief in the efficacy of coaching (that you are really helping people change their lives for the better) and investment (putting time and money into your work feeds your own energy). Continuously expanding your mindset also adds to your work.

Finally, we covered how a strong case of "PC" (project consciousness) can get you to a point where you see coaching and your subject area everywhere. You will then get reminders of it, ideas to improve it, and opportunities to sell yourself as a coach all the time. This project consciousness then becomes a self-energizing mechanism in your life and business.

CHAPTER FIVE
MASTER YOUR COACHING SKILLS

When you have a potential client, defined as someone who is interested in retaining your services as a life coach, it is in your interest to offer a short complimentary coaching session to them.

This free offer has several advantages to both you and the client. First, it establishes you as a person of good will, showing that you are a generous professional. Second, it's a chance for you to showcase your skills. Third, you can provide genuine value, which fuels your soul and reminds you of why you do this work in the first place. Fourth, you get a glimpse into what working with this person would be like. Fifth, you raise the possibility of this individual immediately referring you to their friends.

Within a general thirty-minute session, you could demonstrate your ability to use searching questions about the person's motives. For example:

- What makes you want to pursue a coaching relationship?
- What would you want to accomplish by being coached?
- What would make our coaching relationship a success for you?

Any one of these questions could elicit some good material for you to actively listen, meaning, reflect back the client's response in your own words, emphasizing the feelings you pick up.

After doing this several times, you can move toward selling yourself:

- What would make a great coaching relationship, from your perspective?
- Here's how I would work with you on that goal . . .
- Does this sound like what you are looking for?

Next you will move to close, filling in the details that help move the potential client toward a decision in your favor. Tell them

- how often and how long the sessions will be
- what a typical session looks like
- details regarding calls (Skype, phone, etcetera)
- what the client will be expected to do between sessions
- your fees and how to make payments.
- Don't forget to ask the client to sign up!

Does the idea of sessions make you feel overwhelmed or intimidated? If so, practice you complimentary sessions with a friend or spouse first. Have them act as the potential client and go through the session as a role-play.

Afterward, ask for feedback. Does your friend have comments, criticisms, or suggestions for improving your presentation? Would they have been likely to sign up? What would have made them more comfortable or likely to commit?

UNDERSTANDING: THE BEDROCK OF SUCCESS IN COACHING

*Be kinder than necessary, for everyone
you meet is fighting some kind of battle.*

What satisfies us as human beings? Most people would think of satisfaction as coming either from *having* or *doing*. For instance, regarding having, it satisfies us to own a new house or car, to have friends, a job, health, wealth, etcetera.

On the doing side, we find satisfaction from working to build or accomplish something—completing a project, receiving recognition for an accomplishment, doing well in our profession, or producing something artistic or musical.

All these satisfactions, however, come from doing something that prospers or benefits us. An even deeper satisfaction can be that which comes to us through *giving*.

Whenever we are able to help someone, we feel good. Why? The reason helping others satisfies us is because *it connects us*. We feel that we belong to something larger. Whenever we give help to someone, it brings a joy of connecting us more deeply with that community. If you never contribute to that community, other members of it will never fully feel or appreciate you. But when you do contribute, you experience more than mere satisfaction. It doesn't matter how small the deed of helping; we can still derive happiness from our contribution.

Helping others, it turns out, is also good business. When you start to help others, people will begin to rely on you. You will start building up a bank account of good relationships. The more you help others, the more deposits you make into that account. Once they see you as a good friend, they will recommend you to their associates, remember you in times of need, or look to you as a thought leader. If you have a coaching business, helping others helps you doubly: it gives you deep, repeated satisfaction and it builds your business.

Using my coaching and seminar contact lists, I offered a yearlong course I called Success University. In the meantime, I was doing two seminars a month, coaching clients and writing a book. Despite the satisfaction of achieving these things, the high amount of activity drained me. My energy was lower than ever yet the demands for it were off the charts.

What could I do to have more energy? I began to educate myself in health and wellness and their place in producing a higher quality of life for myself.

I found that not only were good nutrition and exercise important contributors to high energy, but also that there was an Inner Game aspect to it—meditation and mindfulness. This, of course, was right up my alley.

Through constant study—reading, attending seminars, and listening to audio programs—I learned all I could about health and wellness. I listened to and got to know experts on high productivity as well.

Then I followed my favorite strategy: looking at a problem I myself was having, thinking of others who were facing the same thing, and searching for a solution to the problem in marketing terms.

I began to notice that people needed more energy, just like I did. I thought, "I now have the information and the resources to be able to teach them how to have more energy." For the marketing solution, I began designing and offering seminars in wellness and mindfulness.

What is the key principle to learn from this stage of my life? Projection. Take what you are facing in your own life and project it out onto others; then look to see if you are indeed right in assuming the problem is shared.

In my case, I didn't have to look far. I saw people dragging to work each day, exhausted by the weekend, and rushing to catch up on home and family matters with every spare minute they had. They looked the way I felt!

The next obvious step was to do something about it, to find my own answers and then design a way to help others get results by sharing the strategies the best way I knew how to—through marketing life seminars.

- What problem are you facing in your life right now?
- How are you going about seeking a solution to it?
- What research do you need to conduct in order to learn more about the problem?
- How widespread is the problem? How many people are facing it?
- What can you do to offer assistance to them?

In the process of these developments, I was getting to know quite a lot of important people. I was hungry for knowledge, so everywhere I went I talked to people, asked questions, and found out what I could about their secrets of success. In my seeking it seemed that, one by one, different worlds or "games" of opportunity were opening to me. I learned that this newfound area of how to have more energy was such a game, and a lot of people were playing in it.

As I worked on improving my own life, I started to teach others how to do the same and discovered a very receptive audience.

The problems I encountered, however, were with regard to my growth as a businessman. I had a team of people now to help me market, plan, and produce seminars. They were on the phones day and night, making calls to sign people up for the events.

Every month I was worrying: How many sign-ups do we have? Is it enough to move forward? In my hurry and enthusiasm, I pushed my people to produce.

Ironically, I began to notice that the harder I worked, the less sign-ups I produced. In the month of September, only four people signed up.

Seeing this, I thought, "I have to do something radically different here!"

That's when I came across the idea to market through video. My team helped me develop a video to teach quality-of-life skills and simultaneously advertise the seminars. After it went live, my next two-day seminar received fifty sign-ups!

I created a YouTube speech called "Seven Steps to Success" so that even before these individuals attended my event, I was adding value to their life. Suddenly it seemed that I was flying high again.

When you work for yourself, you have to constantly ask: do you run the business or does the business run you? It's easy to get caught up and forget some of the deeper issues. For example, how much am I helping others? And is my desire to serve more clients draining me of the time I need to be alone, with my loved ones, or resting?

Despite my growing success, adversity arrived at my doorstep once again, delivering a critical lesson.

In a single email on a normal work day, I received an email from my team that could be summed up in two words: We. Quit.

I had overworked and underencouraged them to the point of breaking. They were worn out and blamed me, rightly so.

The timing couldn't have been worse. A three-day seminar was approaching and suddenly everything was on my shoulders.

I worked tirelessly to cover all needs and focus 100% on adding value to my attendees.

When the crowds cleared after the final session, people came rushing up to me to say, "Akira, you changed my life this weekend."

Those words nourished my soul and brought my confidence and mood back up. The next day I went to the empty office and sat alone to think.

After an initial period of feeling sorry for myself, I began to ask the empty room, "What can I do? I'm a good seminar leader but I'm not doing well at team building. How can I do better for the people who work with me?"

That's when a massive realization hit me:

"ALWAYS SUPPORT THE PEOPLE WHO SUPPORT YOU."

AKIRA IGUCHI

"Why should people who worked for me get any less of my heart energy and support than my coaching clients?" I asked myself.

I learned from my mistake. I found better people, formed and optimized a new team, and focused on treating them better. I shared with them what I wanted to accomplish, the values I wanted to get across to people, and these became our working values. If there was a problem, my people knew we could sit down together and hammer out a mutually agreeable solution.

Good results began to pour in. We started selling memberships, online products, and joint programs. I began collaborating with other leaders to maximize our impact and seminar attendance while also getting their help with marketing and writing.

DEVELOPING A COACHING AGENDA

It is a good idea to have a client develop a personal profile for you to look over. This helps you get to know and understand the person, plus it can help in creating a coaching agenda. Questions you might ask the client to complete for you could include

- What would you say is your life purpose? Do you have the sense you were "made" to do something or to fulfill a mission? If so, what is it?
- How well do your current roles and activities serve that purpose?
- What are your three most important values?
- What is currently your strongest priority?
- What problem or challenge do you most want to overcome?
- What are five of your strengths? Three weaknesses?

WHAT DOES A COACHING SESSION LOOK LIKE?

I have alluded several times to a general plan for a coaching session. Once you start working with a client, a typical session will begin with greetings, briefly reviewing the goal the client set at the close of the previous session, and asking about their progress in achieving it. This will generally progress into a discussion of a current issue that is standing in the client's way of achieving something. The session will close by agreeing on a new goal and what action steps the client will take to achieve it by the next time you meet.

A popular way of summarizing these steps is the GROW model, based on the Inner Game method developed by Timothy Gallwey. It is a simple method for goal setting and problem solving that was developed in the United Kingdom and used extensively in corporate coaching in the late 1980s and 1990s.

The GROW model consists of the following components:

1. **GOAL:** The goal is the end point, where the client wants to be. The goal has to be defined in such a way that it is very clear to the client when they have achieved it. That may require adding measurable indicators such as pounds, dollars.

2. **REALITY:** The current reality is where the client is now. What are their issues? How far are they away from the goal?

3. **OBSTACLES:** There will be obstacles preventing the client from getting to where they want to go. If there were no obstacles, the client would already have reached

their goal. The "O" also stands for **Options**. These are ways of dealing with and getting beyond the obstacles.

4. **WAY FORWARD:** This is where the options need to be converted into action steps that will get the client to their goal.

Whether or not you use the GROW model, you need to develop a way to make each coaching session deliver maximum impact in terms of empowering the client to face their problems and determining steps to eliminate them.

Before we leave the subject designing a coaching session template, here are some questions you might find useful in guiding your sessions:

- What important things have happened for you since our last session?

- Give me a brief report on your progress and action steps since we last spoke.

- Which action steps from last time do we need to review and make a new plan for?

- What do you want to make sure we talk about today?

- What is a goal you want to accomplish this week?

- What are your action steps to get there?

Through this process, you are building rapport and trust with your clients. Let's look more specifically at how you can do that most effectively. Two key skills—questioning and listening—will be your most commonly used skills.

KEY COACHING SKILL 1: BUILDING RAPPORT

When you're just starting a new client relationship, whether your coaching session is complementary or the first in a series, your immediate concern should be to build rapport with that person.

If your coaching clients are using Skype or some other visual means of communicating, you will want to train them in two different areas regarding their physical presentation: body language and facial expressions. Mastering these two areas will help your clients have incredible rapport with their own clients.

You will help your clients to be more relaxed and trusting if you use open body language. That means your arms are open, your legs are uncrossed, and you're making frequent eye contact. Open body language makes you look relaxed. Subconsciously, this indicates to clients that you're friendly and good-natured.

The next step is to focus on facial expressions.

When I started doing coaching sessions I had a terrible habit of always looking concerned in my sessions. I genuinely was concerned about helping them accomplish their goals, but looking that way seemed to tell a different story. I looked like I was disagreeing with what they were saying. As a result, my clients would start closing their communication and body language.

When I realized that I wasn't smiling very much during sessions, I started to practice subtle smiling as they were explaining to me the goals they wanted to accomplish. This made a dramatic improvement in how much they opened up to me.

When people listen to others they tend not to smile as they listen. Try to make a conscious effort to smile when you communicate with your clients, even when you're listening to them. Don't use a forced smile, but instead share a sincere, friendly one.

Remember that your facial expressions should still be appropriate for the situation. If the client is talking about something uncomfortable or sad, it's not the time to beam widely.

Knowing about and being able to diagnose language patterns is an effective way to build rapport. The three basic language patterns are:

- visual: describing what things look like to the client
- auditory: describing sounds, what the client hears
- tactile: describing how things physically feel

Asking the client to describe an event or experience is a good way to determine their language pattern. Do they use visual, auditory, or feeling words most frequently?

When you know your client's language pattern, you can start using that same pattern to speak to them. If you communicate using the same type of words they're using, you will be able to connect on a deeper level. Immediately they will sense that you are on their wavelength! And the more they feel that you understand them, the more likely they are to follow your guidance and get incredible results.

You want to make it easy on your clients to come back to you again for coaching. The best way to do that is to make a great first impression and ensure they feel uplifted and encouraged when they leave each session.

One of the best ways to make your clients feel comfortable with you in a coaching session is by asking the right questions. Since there are unlimited questions you could ask, you should prepare them in advance. Your questions should be open-ended and provoke insights and opinions that reveal indicators you need to better personalize your program to their needs.

Here are some sample questions you could adopt in such situations:

- What's one important goal of yours?
- Do you think coaching will help you accomplish this? Why?
- What's something you want to accomplish through coaching?

Once a client starts sharing, I focus on their passions. This gives me the groundwork to form a clearer direction and know where to go deeper with them. Usually when people are really passionate about something, it shows on their faces.

If I don't see any excitement or passion, I'll start asking more questions about why they want to do something. I'll just keep asking them why (in different ways) over and over again until they give me an indicator such as a smile or some excitement in their voice.

After a while if I'm still not seeing any excitement, I will explain to them that it doesn't sound like they're very passionate or interested in what they're working toward because they're not demonstrating it. Sometimes I'll even ask them, "I don't really believe you want to do this. Are you sure?"

This usually prompts a response that gives me something to work with. Maybe they'll get a little defensive and start trying to prove to me why they are passionate about their idea. Bingo! That's the information I need!

Furthermore, going through this process helps me be clear on where they are at in the process—either just starting, in progress with a little momentum, or totally driven and almost at the point of accomplishment.

Note that there is a fine line between questioning and judging. People view life through their own lenses and often assume others view the world in the same way. Expressing critical judgment in a coaching session can cause clients to shut down immediately because they feel humiliated or judged. On the other hand, having and expressing a nonjudgmental attitude can help clients feel understood or work through their own thought process.

When people are with a coach they just met recently, they are usually in a fragile state. They may already feel they're being judged and look for any evidence to prove themselves right. In other words, they're on the defensive. When you expect this in advance, you can demonstrate nonjudgment toward your coaching clients to help them relax, open up, and be more transparent with you. This will give you a better understanding of them and improve your ability to work together toward their goals.

The starting place when talking to your clients about their goals is to discover what their limiting beliefs are. Writing these insights down will help you determine where they are in relation to their goal and also the biggest areas where you can help them succeed. Put a star next to the "easy wins" where you can accomplish their desired progress the fastest. Look to these stars when your client is having a hard time and needs some quick progress to stay on track.

When I feel like I understand the explanation of their insights and opinions, I often ask my clients more about their current experience on a specific key topic. Then I have them explain where they are in terms of accomplishing their goals.

It's essential to understand where they are in the process of accomplishing their goals. As their coach, my first job is to help them gain clarity: where are they now and where do they want to go? I'll know when I have clarity because I can pinpoint where they are at in their journey.

Knowing this helps me create a plan and show them the path I'm going to lead them on. They also feel more trusting, reassured, and motivated to come back for another session.

KEY COACHING SKILL 2: ASKING QUESTIONS

Questioning is the coach's key skillset. Why? First of all, the questions are focused on the client's favorite subject: themselves. Secondly, when people are asked an important question about themselves, it causes them to think. They have to create answers, to apply their creative ability to the problem. By questioning the client, the coach honors their thinking. A particular value for the coach who asks questions is that he or she has the opportunity to see how smart and capable the client is. When that realization is communicated to the client, it empowers them. Remember that, often, people have some understanding of what they should do and then use a coach's support to reassure them that the decision they're leaning toward is right for them.

Of course, there are questions and there are questions. Questions that seem to demand simple "yes" or "no" answers, called "closed" questions, are not very useful in the coaching process. Instead, rely upon open-ended questions that cause the client to explore his or her thinking.

Don't be afraid of silences in these situations. Brief interludes of no talk at all allow both coach and client to step back and collect their thoughts. As the coach, you can use this time to decide what to ask next and the client can use it to process their answers. Both are valuable.

Breaking the Ice

"How are you today?" "How are things going?" These are common expressions when people meet and start a conversation, but they usually don't expect answers. When you get started with a client and use one of these icebreakers, follow up with another question such as "What makes this a good day?" Or "What's been the high point so far?" Well-worded and well-directed questions can encourage a client to begin thinking introspectively.

Here are some more examples you could use:

- Tell me a little bit about yourself.

- What would people say is most special about you?

- What's the most important thing that's happened to you in the last month?

Rather than talking a lot about what you'll be doing with a new client, spend time at first finding out what they want and what they care about. This shows the client you are genuinely interested in them. For example,

- What's on your mind these days?

- What's a passion of yours?

- What's your dream?

Your client has hired you as their coach for a reason. Having a dream to reach for or wanting to work through a difficult situation are possible reasons. You can move toward what the client wants to accomplish with questions such as:

- What do you hope to gain by working together?
- What challenges are you facing?
- What is an important objective for you right now?
- What seems to be preventing you from achieving that?

KEY COACHING SKILL 3: ACTIVE LISTENING

Carl Rogers, another 1970s industry maker and psychologist, led the practice of "client-centered" approaches to therapy and education. He instigated the widespread training of "active listening" as a means of responding to speakers. This nondirective approach to interaction is one of the most powerful I have ever encountered.

Active listening, also known as nondirective listening or empathic listening, requires a certain level of self-discipline because most listeners spend their listening time thinking of things to say as soon as the speaker concludes. When their mind wanders, the active-listener coach must recenter it on what is being said. Otherwise, important feelings might be missed or overlooked.

This form of interaction consists of listening to what is "behind" the speaker's words, for example, the feelings or bias being expressed. Once the coach understands what those unspoken feelings are, he or she tentatively feeds that feeling back in their own words. In this method, it is important that the listener *paraphrase* what they have heard so to avoid sounding like they are mimicking the speaker. When the feedback is correct, the client immediately feels understood.

The following sentence stems can be useful in providing active-listening feedback:

- "It sounds like you're feeling . . ."
- "In other words . . ."
- "Is this what you are saying . . . ?"
- "I'm sensing that you . . ."
- "Sounds like that felt to you . . ."
- "So, when that happened, you felt . . ."
- "Tell me more about . . ."

Note that the emphasis is more on feelings than facts and the feedback is tentative. This creates an aura of "I could be wrong about this" and inviting correction on the speaker's part.

Of course, the coach should not continue this style of feedback indefinitely. In a typical coaching session, listening is a tool for uncovering where to go next, so it often leads to action planning.

After the client's feelings have been expressed, often there is relief from their grip on his or her thinking, and a decision or plan of action opens up where one was previously hidden. It is often useful to use the client's own key words, especially those that appear important to him or her, in active listening feeding. This builds mutual understanding and keeps things on track.

Now that we've covered the most productive ways to be an active listener, here are several responses that should be avoided. These responses can block the communication and inhibit mutual understanding when the coach use in them: *criticizing, interpreting, praising, deriding, advising, analyzing, teasing, minimizing feelings, or telling their own story.* These responses on the part of the coach can raise barriers to the client's flow of thought and speech. They are responses not to the client's needs but to the coach's needs.

The difference between questioning and active listening should be clear. In the first style, when you question a client ("Why do you feel that way?" or "What have you tried so far?" or "Do you have a plan?") you are seeking information. In the second style, when you employ active listening, you are promoting understanding through clarification.

To summarize, active listening:

- helps clarify the way the client feels
- is a tool for demonstrating the coach's understanding of the client
- promotes trust and goodwill between coach and client
- is a tool for bringing self-understanding to the client
- is not to be confused with analysis or therapy
- keeps the coach in the role of a responder and supporter, rather than an advisor
- builds trust and confidence
- helps pave the way to decision making and action.

Listening as a Marketing Tool

Active listening is an important tool, not only in working with clients, but also in finding them. In other words, listening is a powerful marketing tool. When you put yourself in a variety of environments to interact with others, listening can be a more important skill than speaking.

Many people perceive marketing as initiating conversations, giving information, or "talking at people." I don't believe this is the most effective way to market.

Instead, I believe in being a great listener. When you can accomplish this, the world will beat a path to your door because everyone wants an understanding ear. If you are talking all the time, it does not advertise you well as a coach. By contrast, if you listen well and *demonstrate your understanding* of others, they will see you as a worthy coach.

If it helps you, think of each of your meet-ups as an opportunity to demonstrate your coaching skill "free of charge." When someone at a dinner party finds you to be a willing and understanding listener who doesn't seek to take their turn but gives time and attention to others, he or she will walk away thinking, "That person listened to me so well. I can see what a benefit I would get from having such a coach. I think I will give them a call!"

Putting the Key Skills Together

Questioning and listening belong together in the coach's tool kit, ever ready during a coaching session. Remember that coaching is not about you, the coach, but rather about them, the client. Therefore, these skills should be constantly in use during a session. Let's look at how this might work.

Coach:	Tell me about what's going on with you. *(Question or cue)*
Client:	Well, I've been trying to devote some time on weekends to starting my coaching business but I can't say it's going well.
Coach:	It sounds like you're frustrated because something isn't working. *(Active listening, feeding back)*

Client:	Right.
Coach:	So, what's in the way? *(Questioning, seeking information)*
Client:	My son's ballgames. He has a game every Saturday. It takes pretty much all of my day when the game is in another town.
Coach:	I see. So your Saturdays are pretty much locked up. *(Listening, reviewing)* What else could you try? *(Questioning, cueing)*
Client:	I guess I could take some time on Sunday.
Coach:	Would that work? . . . etc.

Skillful use of questioning and active listening not only keeps the conversation moving but also enables the coach to keep the focus on the client, their issue, and what they can do about it. All this moves the conversation eventually toward your agreement on the setting of a new goal for the week ahead before the session ends.

COACHING MODEL: Learning Styles

Learning styles are common ways that people learn. While everyone has a mix of learning styles, most people may find that they have one dominant style with far less usage of the others. You may discover that you employ different styles in different circumstances. There is no "correct" mix, nor is your style fixed. You can develop ability in less dominant styles as well as further develop styles that you already use well.

Using multiple learning styles is a relatively new approach that educators have only recently started to recognize. Traditional schooling employed (and continues to employ) a limited range of learning and teaching techniques such as relying on linguistic and logical teaching methods.

By recognizing and understanding your own learning styles, you can use techniques better suited to you. This improves the speed and quality of your learning.

Most researchers agree there are seven different learning styles:

1. visual (spatial)
2. aural (auditory or musical)
3. verbal (linguistic)
4. physical (kinesthetic)
5. logical (mathematical)
6. social (interpersonal)
7. solitary (intrapersonal)

A client's learning style guides the way he or she learns. They also change the way they internally represent experiences, the way they recall information, and even the words they choose.

Research shows that each learning style uses different parts of the brain. By involving more of the brain during learning, we remember more of what we learn.

Researchers using brain-imaging technologies have been able to find out the key areas of the brain responsible for each learning style. For example, while the occipital lobes at the back of the brain manage the visual sense, the temporal lobes handle aural content (this is why the right temporal lobe is especially important for music). The temporal and frontal lobes are engaged in verbal learning and the cerebellum and motor cortex handle much of our physical movement. The parietal lobes, especially the left side, drive our logical thinking while the frontal and temporal lobes handle much of our social activities. The limbic system, which has a lot to do with emotions, moods, and aggression, also influences the social style. The frontal and parietal lobes and the limbic system are active with the solitary style. By recognizing and understanding your own learning styles, you can use techniques better suited to you. This improves the speed and quality of your learning.

DEALING WITH A CLIENT'S LIMITING BELIEFS

When you have your first coaching client, a lot of time will be spent focusing on gathering insight about why the client has or hasn't accomplished their goal yet. Usually the justification is an obstacle or *belief* that an obstacle exists, so you will need to focus on asking key questions that will help your client identify these obstacles in their current situation.

It's important to remember that we are coaches and not therapists. In the process of helping people achieve their goals, we are going to listen to a lot of frustration. As a coach, when you hear limiting beliefs and frustrations, you must be prepared with responses. Since your responses will be specific to your client, it's best that you come up with responses each client can connect with.

When I hear someone share a limiting belief such as "I can't see myself ever being able to make more money," I ask, "Do you have to be able to see something for it to be possible?"

Other times, I ask them a question that makes them think in a different way. For example, "What are ways you can make more money as a coach?" This eliminates the option to produce another negative response.

To give you a greater explanation of this concept in practice, I will share a story with you from my own experience.

"Steve" (as I'll call him) wanted to pursue his passion for learning piano but every hour he spent practicing was an hour he felt that he was neglecting his family.

In our sessions, Steve would repeat the same limiting beliefs about why he could never pursue his passion. In the beginning, he could list almost twenty reasons in a row! Hearing this, I understood my job as his coach was to enable him to break through this mental barrier.

I then asked him the question, "How can you pursue your passion when all you think about are reasons why you cannot? You've done a great job of giving me twenty reasons why you can't pursue your passion. Now, can you try to think of twenty reasons why you can?"

At first Steve insisted that was impossible. Then, after working together for several minutes, I steered him away from his negative thoughts until he understood that his greatest obstacle was focusing on his limiting beliefs.

One by one, Steve listed all twenty reasons why he could play piano. Suddenly, he felt like a whole world of new opportunities was open to him!

He soon realized he was not being selfish or neglecting his family. Rather, he had their support because they saw he was pursuing something he was truly passionate about.

Steve went on to pursue his dreams. He released his doubt, stopped making excuses, and followed the stepping-stones we laid to lead him toward success.

"Steve" is my favorite type of coaching client because he came to me with his concerns and openly sought my guidance. When someone is receptive and open minded, it makes the process and transition seamless.

As I did with Steve, you must use questions to gain insights into your client's goals and then active listening to clarify the experiences they've had in pursuing those goals. This insight will help you tear down disabling beliefs and create new belief patterns to support your client's goals. A quick review of the section in chapter 2 called "Managing Self-Talk" is in order here. Now that you know about killer statements and how they work to reduce motivation and confidence, you can be on the lookout for such attitudes in your clients.

CHAPTER SUMMARY

As a coach, you have the good fortune of making an income through helping others. You enable them to overcome barriers, bring out and recognize their own skills, and create a better life for themselves in the process.

A typical coaching session opens with a review of the last goal that was set and the client's reporting of the progress they made toward achieving it.

During the session, new issues will be explored that are current in the client's experience. You and the client will choose one of these to work on, discuss it, and set a goal to address and overcome it.

The session ends when the two of you agree on steps the client will take between now and the next session to accomplish this.

The coach's most used and powerful skills in a typical coaching session are questioning and active listening. Questions are designed to help the client search within and elicit responses. Active listening includes paraphrasing the client's statements in an effort to clarify or uncover expressed and unexpressed feelings. This strategy builds rapport, trust, and understanding between the coach and client by going beyond the facts the client is reporting and showing that the coach understands the client at a deeper level.

Knowledge of learning styles can give the coach a deeper insight into the client's preferences for learning, thinking, changing, and growing. By altering their coaching method to incorporate these preferences, the coach can be more effective and increase client satisfaction.

CHAPTER SIX

FINDING PEOPLE TO SERVE

I magine answering your phone to hear, "Hello. I've been thinking I need a coach in my life and you came highly recommend. I'd like to hear about your style, fees, and availability."

That would be a nice call, right? How did these prospective clients come to hear about your services? Most commonly, it is through prospecting.

WHAT IS PROSPECTING?

Every business needs customers to survive. Prospecting is a large part of the coaching business as you create relationships with new clients and affiliates.

One of the most frequent questions I'm asked is why prospecting is so important. The simple answer is that it makes it easier to develop relationships online.

Are you getting intimidated? Remain calm! Most people are initially resistant to prospecting. They associate pain with the process because they have to talk to new people and proactively follow up. The best cure for this is to practice until it becomes second nature. As coaches, you (and your clients!) must get over any fear of talking to people.

The truth is, the faster you become skilled at prospecting, the better you will perform. In fact, I believe there is a direct relationship between prospecting skills and your success as a coach. Great prospecting skills almost always translate into more clients, higher income and greater consistency. Needless to say, these skills are critical to your coaching success!

KEEPING IT IN THE FAMILY

When it comes to developing your prospecting skills, it is essential to note what's working to solidify new connections and what isn't.

When I was starting out, I barely spoke any English and it was extremely difficult for me to strike up a conversation with someone new. It was also difficult to be engaged in conversations and know what questions to ask. Had I stayed in my comfort zone and not pushed myself to engage, I wouldn't be where I am today. I would probably still be a waiter in a restaurant. Having the ability to meet, engage, and develop relationships with people will open more doors for you and your clients than you can imagine. This is how successful companies are built.

So where can you prospect for clients? The short answer is: everywhere. I've already talked about prospecting with family, friends, and associates. Now I will focus on three areas that make prospecting easier: special groups, small businesses, and the Chamber of Commerce.

Let's start with special groups. Almost every town has a place where groups meet to exchange ideas, opinions, and information. This could be something as simple as a church group, a book club, or even a poker night with buddies.

When approaching a special group to prospect, the first step is simply to show up. Don't force a prospecting pitch on the first day unless it comes naturally. No one likes the "new guy" who "just shows up to sell us something." Instead, start mingling and asking others questions about themselves and their interests.

When I go to a new group event, I try to meet one person right away. Then, I ask if they know anybody else in the room. If they don't, I'll talk to them for a few minutes and then go meet someone else. I will then talk to that person for a few minutes before introducing the second person to the first person.

I repeat this practice all night to meet more people and give the appearance of being well connected. I'm generally able to talk to and acknowledge everyone I meet for the rest of the night and from that point on. When I attend the same event the following week, chances are I already know most of the people there.

If anyone new shows up, I reach out and introduce them to a few people. This makes the new individual feel great and puts you at the center of the social circle.

At this point in my familiarity of the group, I work to start deepening my connections.

This next strategy is a tried and true way for your coaching clients to connect with small businesses. A story about my friend Rob is a perfect illustration. Rob grew up in a small town in Colorado and he was a natural communicator. On an average day, he would walk into a small business and introduce himself. After he got to know the owner, he would introduce him to others in the same building. He repeatedly connected people for so many years that eventually he couldn't walk into town without being recognized.

You can follow Rob's example simply by walking into small shops, meeting the owners, and connecting them with others. By repeating this process, you will grow your network and become regarded as someone who knows everyone and connects people.

The third approach is through your local Chamber of Commerce. Most chapters have "leads groups" where participants attend primarily to do exactly that—get leads.

Want to know the secret to prospecting these groups? Show up and give leads instead. By finding out what each of the business owners wants and spending time helping them get leads, you will develop a reputation for having an amazing work ethic and being generous.

Notice we haven't discussed directly prospecting these three areas yet. Here's the reason: we're creating value first and then prospecting.

The final area I want cover is prospecting with family, friends, and coworkers. You must start reaching out to your family today. Call them out of the blue, just to see how they're doing. Tell them that you are thinking about them and see if there's anything going on in their life. Do the same with friends and coworkers you haven't talked to in a while. Even texting can be effective. The idea is to talk at least one or two times this month before offering free coaching sessions.

After all, even though you probably have good relationships with family, friends, and coworkers, the focus must always be on providing value first.

Just like your clients did at the leads groups, they should focus on providing value before asking for anything. Asking first always makes the experience feel transactional, and that approach can lead to shallow connections. Using this approach leads to deep and meaningful relationships—the exact kinds of relationships you must focus on building.

Having met amazing new people, it's time to start offering free coaching sessions. Using this approach pays great dividends. Most of these new connections are generally happy to have a free coaching session with you because they've already seen the value you've provided over the past four weeks.

After the first session, ask the individual for both feedback and referrals. All you have to say is: "Thank you so much for participating in this free coaching session. Do you know anyone else who is as passionate about [insert your topic area here] as you? It would be great if you could introduce me over Facebook. Who do you think would be most interested?"

As soon as you've asked this question, wait quietly. While your prospective client comes up with the name, pull out your phone and open Facebook. Click on the search field, hand them your phone and say, "Please friend me on Facebook. We can do the introduction there."

They will then add you as a friend and follow up on the referral. If they haven't introduced you in five to seven days, just say, "Hey, do you have a moment today to introduce me to your friend that likes travel?" At that point, if you get the referral, it's great. If not, just move on. You never know if that contact will send you someone at a future time.

PROSPECTING ON SOCIAL MEDIA

Online prospecting is one of the most powerful ways for you and your clients to grow your businesses. If I lost all my money needed to pay rent, I would go straight to social media to drum up some business.

The following principles apply to practically any social media website. For the sake of simplicity, I'll use the examples of Facebook, LinkedIn, and Twitter.

When prospecting on a given platform, remember the purpose of that platform. Here are the most common ones:

- Facebook focuses on connecting family and friends.

- LinkedIn focuses on making business-related connections.

- Twitter is used to share news and follow interests.

- Instagram is about sharing photos and having conversations around them.

NOTE: Although Instagram and YouTube are definitely popular social media platforms, your clients' time is better spent elsewhere when it comes to drumming up new prospects.

Even though you can use these sites for purposes other than those stated above, they may be less effective. You need to focus on using each platform for its designated purpose. Please don't join the population of people wasting months of their time creating things that are not appropriate for their platform.

Not only is online prospecting effective, it can be incredibly efficient. Once when I didn't have many coaching clients, I was $400 short of making my rent. I had three days to make the payment before being evicted.

Not knowing what to do, I began surfing through social media, asking, "How can I get a coaching client on Facebook?" I started reaching out to dozens of friends and family and reminding them that I was really good at coaching on how to find one's passions. I offered that service for twenty dollars.

Within hours, several people showed interest. In just under two days, over twenty people had sent me twenty dollars.

Stories of time-crunched successful prospecting on social media are everywhere. In fact, dozens of my students have shared such stories with me personally.

Facebook

You probably already have a Facebook account, but is your Facebook profile set-up in the right way?

I'm not talking about fan pages but rather a personal profile page. After all, your social media personal profile is your billboard to the world.

The most important part of your page is the content. You need to look professional. It's okay to have pictures of family and friends, but remember clients will see everything they post. Since most online prospecting will occur on your Facebook page, it's best to unpublish or hide any unprofessional images or other content that might detract from your image.

The story of a coaching client is a good example of the influence of poor social media branding and how you can recover.

One coaching client had dozens of posts of him smoking, drinking, and partying with friends. He also had a lot of profanity and politi-

cal rhetoric. Potential clients looked at his page and turned the other way thinking, "Who would want to hire this guy?" I, too, was surprised. When I spoke to him, he seemed like a normal, agreeable guy.

If you're worried about falling into this same category, just take the time tonight to clean up your page.

After my friend followed my recommendation to delete all the questionable pictures and videos, he started posting about his family, pets, and values. This small change made a massive difference in his appeal to potential clients. He went from looking like a frat kid touring the party circuit to a professional family man who was going places.

After updating your Facebook page, go through and consider or ask for feedback regarding anything that should be added. These are some of the most essential functions on Facebook that you can use to your advantage:

- Featured photos: These photos can be added to a profile by clicking "Add Featured Photos" just below your profile picture. If you've already added featured photos, hover over the section and click the pencil icon in the top right corner. Then, click the photo icon and select the desired photo.

- Bio: A short bio can be added to a profile by going to your profile and clicking "Add a Short Bio." You can also edit this by clicking the pencil icon in that section.

- Family members: Add your relatives to your profile by going to the profile page, then clicking on "Family and Relationships" and "Add a Family Member." Be sure to save your changes.

- About page: Content can be added to your "About" page by going to the profile page, clicking "About" below the cover photo, and scrolling to the specific section you want to change.

- Hidden content: Content such as movies, music, and TV can be hidden by going to your profile page, clicking on "About," hovering over the content you want to hide until the cursor turns into a pencil, then selecting "Hide from Section."

One of the best uses of Facebook is reconnecting with people you haven't spoken to in a while. I always start by sending a personalized message to each person on my entire friends list. This usually takes about a week for every few hundred friends. Focus on creating conversations around what their friends and family are doing now and what excites them about their future. Go into more detailed questions after you feel that you've rekindled the friendship.

If they ask what you've been doing, I let them know right away that you are coaching and that one of your goals is to connect more with friends and develop meaningful relationships. This becomes a great conversation starter.

Another technique I have found effective on Facebook is sharing related content. For example, if I come across an article that pertains to one of my friend's areas of interest, I will share it and then tag them with a note.

This way, my friend will be notified that they've been mentioned in their notifications. If the person isn't on your friends list, type an "@" symbol followed by their Facebook name, and click on their picture when it comes up.

One of my clients, Marius, put this technique to very effective use when he reconnected with a friend, Maria, on Facebook. In their discussion, he learned that they share an interest in food gardening but Maria lives in an arctic climate.

When Marius found an article about how to grow an avocado tree in any climate he posted it to Facebook and tagged Maria. The thoughtful action kept their discussion going and reinforced their relationship.

After you've restarted relationships online, start asking people out for coffee. If they don't live nearby, invite them to keep the dialogue open.

Then for the next month, start sending one-sentence updates or communications to them. For example, "Have a great weekend, Jim. I'm doing X. What are you doing?" This shows the person that you were thinking about them, not as a prospect but as a friend. Once the relationship is rekindled, it's easier to ask them who they know that might be interested in your coaching services.

LinkedIn

Let's discuss how to drum up business on LinkedIn now.

The intent of LinkedIn is to develop business connections, which is why most profiles read like online résumés. Naturally, then, your first task is to build up an impressive profile that highlights your strengths and presents you as a highly regarded coach.

From there, as with Facebook, the second step is to connect with the people you know—family, friends, and former coworkers. The more people you connect with, the more people you can potentially reach.

The third step is to learn about the people you're trying to connect with. With a completed profile, you can learn a lot of personal information about a friend or prospect. This information is especially useful when making new connections because it provides a topic to start a discussion. Let the conversation grow from there.

An incredibly useful feature of LinkedIn is the ability to see who has recently viewed your profile. Use the "Who's viewed my profile?" function to begin. The fact that someone has looked at your profile is a perfect excuse to connect with them, in my eyes. Even if that person isn't interested in your coaching services, they might *know someone* who is.

As with in-person networking, *you must present value* when building these new relationships through LinkedIn. By first being a resource to others, you establish that you are trustworthy, helpful, and generous—in other words, the type of person others want to be around.

Twitter

Finally, let's cover how to put the buzz bird—Twitter—to work in your business? Unless your client is a celebrity, prospecting over Twitter can be challenging. That said, Twitter is the perfect resource for you to stay on top of your niches.

By subscribing to the feed of the thought leaders in and around your niches, you're assured to always be up to date on the latest and greatest in your field. You must constantly grow and offer more value to your clients. Twitter can act as a barometer for what's hot and what people want to know, informing your offers and blog topics.

Beyond staying informed, Twitter can offer a great path to staying fresh in the minds of your clients. By posting something share-worthy on a consistent basis, you will keep your clients and followers engaged. While Twitter might not be the best place to prospect, it's a great way to stay current with the latest trends and also broadcast valuable information.

Social media can be one of the most efficient mediums for prospecting when you know how to harness its power.

THE ELEVATOR PITCH

As you get started, the greatest advertisement of your coaching business will come directly from you. That's why crafting and solidifying an impactful elevator pitch is so critical. Just like the name implies, it must be short enough to deliver in a brief elevator ride with your listener. It's a clear, short commercial about you and your goals as a coach.

In order to get your pitch just right, you'll likely need to go through several versions. Focus on making it sound compelling yet natural when delivered in a conversation.

You'll need to tailor your pitch according to what you need to convey and who you are trying to target. Start by thinking about the objective of your pitch. For instance, do you want to tell potential clients about your passion? Do you have a particular skill set you want to highlight? Or do you want a simple and engaging way to convince them that they need a coach?

Since many people aren't familiar with life coaching, start your pitch by describing who life coaching is for and what it does. Focus on the problems you help your clients solve and add information or a statistic that shows the value in what you do.

Let's walk through an example to illustrate further. Assume you're in an airport and have just bumped into a former associate. After a few hellos, they ask, "What are you up to these days?" You might answer:

"I'm doing well as a life coach, getting a lot of satisfaction out of helping clients achieve their goals and working through obstacles holding them back from living a more fulfilling life."

If your friend has to catch their plane, you might add, "So good to see you. Here's my card. If you know anyone who could use a coach, will you have them give me a call?"

PRESENTING THE BENEFITS OF COACHING

Another common means of reaching new prospects is through public presentations. Speaking before a group of people allows them a firsthand look at your style, ideas, and values. Always be ready, no matter how small or informal the meeting is, to sign someone up at the end of your talk.

Imagine you have just been introduced to an audience that wants to hear about coaching. After introducing yourself briefly, consider saying something like:

Hi, I'm _____(your name)_____, and I'm a life coach. One of my favorite questions to ask my coaching clients is "What's your dream?" I'm fascinated to hear what people would like to do with their lives, but also I am struck by the fact that no one has ever turned me down. So I am going to make an educated guess right now about you, my audience. I'm betting that each one of you has a dream. Maybe you don't think about it much, but I'm asking you right now: If you were in a position to do anything you wanted with your life, what would it be?

(Pause.)

Now, I imagine some little voices are answering my question in your head. I hope I'm wrong, but maybe those voices are saying, "Well, forget it. My dream is not going to happen. Pipe dream, that's what it is! Given my situation, my limits, my responsibilities, I could never do that, so why even think about it? Blah, blah, blah."

Just for now, if you do have a little negative voice like that going off in your head, I'm going to ask you not to listen to it. I'm going to ask you to ask instead, "Why not? After all, this is your cherished ideal you're considering!"

Let yourself dwell for a moment on what it would be like to realize that dream in your life. Now think about looking back on your accomplishments and seeing that all along the way to achieving them you had a partner, a life coach who was fully dedicated to getting you there.

Now, maybe you've never heard of life coaching. That's an umbrella term that encompasses coaching for any number of topics from relationships to finances to cultivating healthy habits.

Life coaching is very popular with people of all ages throughout the world. Coaches and clients can be in different places since most coaching sessions take place over phone or Skype. There are life coaches for every age group, life stage, ambition, and goal you can imagine.

Life coaching is a process that requires the full commitment of the client. Coaches help clients identify blocks, challenges, and opportunities. Additionally, many life coaches are very accomplished in their own lives and are good at asking key questions to unlock their client's potential.

There is a saying, "The quality of your life is a function of the quality of questions you ask yourself." Great life coaches know how to ask you the questions that will evoke the kind of answers that elevate the quality of your life. A coach will work with you over a set period of time to make sure you follow through on your commitments since accountability is built into the coaching process.

So what is the number one reason to hire a life coach? This may seem like an odd answer, but I would say that it's to develop better relationships with your loved ones. That's the payoff for choosing to work with a professional who supports you in achieving your life goals. Working with a life coach means that you are taking full responsibility for your life going forward. This releases the energy caught up in past disappointments, resentments, and bitterness.

When you take time and effort to give yourself a chance to create the life you desire and see actual results, I guarantee you will develop a greater appreciation for life and those around you. Your positive energy will influence how you relate to your loved ones. Your real life results may even inspire those around you to pursue their own goals. Your newfound energy, appreciation, and sense of responsibility will elevate the quality of your relationships. It will also mean that you remove the pressure you may have been putting on others to offer you advice, support, and accountability for your goals, so the time you spend with your loved ones can be focused on enjoying and truly appreciating each person exactly as they are.

So if achieving some of your authentic life goals results in your creating deeper, more meaningful relationships with those you love, then those life coaching sessions are probably worth much more than the specific goals you hired them for in the first place. Any questions?

Such a short, to-the-point presentation will probably evoke a lot of questions from your listeners. Most of these questions should be routine ones that you can predict and use to move your audience members toward signing up as your coaching clients.

Where might this stand-up presentation take place? Maybe in someone's living room or maybe in a club, church, community or professional meeting. Take steps to get yourself on the agenda as a guest presenter and find groups that are willing and enthusiastic about hearing from you about your Lifestyle Millionaire Coaching business.

PROSPECTING ON SOCIAL MEDIA

Social media makes it incredibly easy to find people with whom you've fallen out of touch. It's also easy to find friends of friends, as well as groups of people who are focused on topics related to your coaching clients' niches. You need to treat building relationships via social media the same way as meeting in person: that is, to be genuine, personal, interesting, and likeable. You can build your social media presence by thinking about your own answers to the following questions:

- What are five visual aspects your profile should include to best represent you and your coaching practice?

- What are three ways you can approach people on social media that invites a relationship?

- What are three ways you can introduce what you do into these relationships without coming off like someone trying to sell something?

- What are three specific ways your clients should become active on Facebook groups?

- What are ten Facebook groups where you should become active?

- How can you effectively use Twitter to further your social media presence?

- How can you effectively use LinkedIn to further your social media presence?

OTHER GREAT APPS YOUR CLIENTS CAN USE FOR PROSPECTING

It's essential that you explore multiple avenues when prospecting, especially in the beginning! This gives you not only more exposure but also more opportunity to discover what's effective. Eventually you will focus your energy into fewer areas—the ones that have proven effective. These questions are aimed at additional ways to help you branch out.

- What are the top three ways you can use Nearby (wnmlive.com)?

- What are the top three ways you can use Meetup (meetup.com)?

- What are the top three ways you can use Nextdoor (nextdoor.com)?

- What are three other sites that are relevant to your interests and local area and how can you best use them?

When I first started out, I knew that coaching consisted largely of asking questions. Not just any questions, the right questions. In order to learn the skill of knowing what to ask a client, one resource helped me a lot. It's called Neuro-Linguistic Programming, or NLP. This system describes the fundamental dynamics between mind (neuro) and language (linguistic) and how their interplay affects our body and behavior (programming). It's about self-discovery, exploring identity and mission. And it provides a framework for understanding the spiritual part of human beings.

As usual with something new to me, I was fascinated. Also as usual, I didn't just dabble in it—I jumped in with both feet. I took an NLP certification class and became a practitioner. This helped me tune in to my clients, to see where they were and where they needed to go.

NLP techniques were important but I soon learned that there is something beyond technique that makes a good coach. It's what I've been emphasizing all throughout this book, the same thing that make you not only a good entrepreneur but also a good person.

I went to one of the top consultants in Japan and asked him what he thought was important, what it took to be a good coach. He told me what I was already learning: "Be present with a client. Truly care about them. Be genuine. Make an emotional connection." There just is no substitute for these qualities, not even technique.

It's the same with goal setting. As a coach you will always be supporting clients in setting goals and achieving them. Achieving a goal is important, *but more important is what happens to you in the process of achieving it.* That's what makes coaching based on teaching people to fish!

I was getting better and getting more clients. I was learning to care about my clients' success—often more than even they did! I also became skilled at rekindling a fire under disillusioned clients, getting them back to a point of enthusiasm about their goal.

And as I did, I opened my heart more to them. As you know from my early years, I wasn't naturally good at coaching or speaking. But I was something else—consistent.

Developing habits of consistency and success were simple but powerful for me. Keep learning. Take action immediately. Be bold. If you keep doing something over and over, you will succeed at it. So it may take months, or a year, but eventually you will master it. And when you do, you yourself are changed by that success. It fits you for the next challenge. These things that I was finding out for myself through personal experience all found their way into the ways I coached my clients.

"NO MATTER HOW SMALL YOU START, START SOMETHING THAT MATTERS."

BRENDON BURCHARD

Early in my career I learned to look for a strategy. There is a strategy for everything, whether it's making money, learning a language, or being a good parent. So, beginning with NLP, I became a strategy collector. And I taught my clients the same thing: Find a strategy. Somebody's already overcome the thing that you are up against, so find that person. Of course, the easiest place to start is with Google!

COACHING MODEL: Change Creates Prospects

Every day, you are coping with change. Change is the modern way of life, whether it's through technology, relationships at work, family issues, or community, all of us have to be ready to shift gears at a moment's notice.

In one sense, change is the coach's blessing because people often need help coping with the changes occurring in their work, health, relationships, finances, etcetera.

I'd like to introduce you now to a model of change that I've found helpful in diagnosing where people are at in the process of coping with a major change. It looks like the letter "S" turned on its side. The lines on either side of the change represent stability that prevails, previous to and following the occurrence of the change.

A BRIEF HISTORY OF CHANGE

Fifty or sixty years ago, changes (represented by the S-shaped curves in the model below) were few and far between. There were long periods of consistent calm between them, so life then felt a lot slower than it does today.

1960s

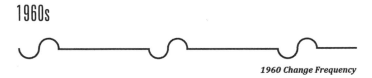

1960 Change Frequency

In the seventies, especially because of technology, changes became more frequent and the periods of stability shorter.

1970s

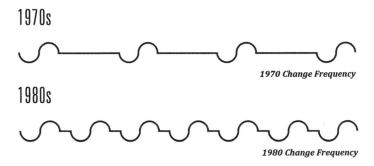

1970 Change Frequency

1980s

1980 Change Frequency

By the nineties, the elongated periods of stability had all but disappeared.

1990s

1990 Change Frequency

By the twenty-first century, the changes were running into each other. When you look at the model below, notice how it resembles a white-water river. This constant turbulence is what we are living with today.

2000s

2000 Change Frequency

When it comes to finding coaching clients, the continual presence of change represents a business opportunity. As discussed, people need help and great coaches when working through changes. This is especially true when they are facing what I call Monster Changes, or MC's.

In our model series, an MC might stick out like this:

Example of a Monster Change

Beyond the day-to-day changes we all endure, certain life events come can place us under intense pressure. These are the Monster Changes, such as marriage, childbirth, new jobs, changing residences, or launching a business.

While these changes may appear to be desirable, usually each of them is difficult to face alone. Actually, it can be terrifying and disorientating to undergo such radical change. In a real sense, the person is letting go of the "old" him or her and taking on a brand new identity—but they haven't reached their new state of stability yet!

Letting go of what you know can be painful and frightening, especially if you think you "should" be happy and are not. A great life coach can help such a client navigate through the change and support them in moving forward in a healthier, more enjoyable way.

Markets constantly change and evolve. To stay on top of their niche, your clients must constantly reinvent themselves. This means that your coaching practices will also need to evolve over time. In fact, the better your ability to adapt to change, the more successful your business will be. The following questions will help you discover where you've been, where you want to go, and how to get there. (You can even use this list of questions to assist your client through their own turbulence.)

1. What are the five biggest changes you've made over the past ten years?

2. What are the top five goals you want to accomplish in the next ten years?

3. What are ten skills you can develop that will increase the amount of value you offer as a coach?

4. Choose the top five items from the previous list and write out the steps you need to take to develop those skills.

5. Choose the top goal from the previous list and write out the exact steps you need to take to start working toward that goal TODAY.

COACHING BUSINESS LEADERS

Coaching is one of the fastest-growing tools in use in business today. According to a Harvard research study, personal coaching has not only become more mainstream in recent years but is considered a "badge of honor." That's because studies are proving the value of coaching in enhancing the performance of executives and companies.

Forty years ago, no one talked about executive coaching. Today, coaching is a popular and potent solution for ensuring top performance from an organization's most critical talent. Coaching supports leaders in developing their emotional intelligence, enhancing team performance, and establishing the fastest path from ideas to execution to increased results.

Having a background in business helps, but it's not a prerequisite if you want to go after the lucrative market of executive coaching. Ask your friends who work in businesses around you to assist you in opening doors to deliver a presentation on coaching to a managerial team. Start with middle managers or team leaders and work your way up. You can probably charge larger fees with these clients than with others in your private practice, since in most cases. companies will pick up the tab.

The purpose of your presentation on coaching is to get new coaching clients. When you win corporate clients, here are some key questions to ask during your initial meeting:

- What's the best thing about working for the organization?
- What's the greatest challenge in working there?
- What happened this month in your sphere of influence as a leader that you feel good about?

- What has to happen for you to move your team to the next level?

- Why do you care about this organization?

- How does this job bring out the best in you?

CHAPTER SUMMARY

Prospecting is the lifeblood of your coaching business. Diligent prospecting requires putting yourself out there, continuously meeting new people, building relationships, and adding value even before asking for leads or business.

Prospects are everywhere. You can start with family and friends by introducing yourself as a coach and offering complimentary sessions to start. Attending clubs, chamber meetings, leads groups, and other group events can be an excellent way to build contacts and add value in a casual environment. Social media can also be a made-to-order method of prospecting.

Speaking to business groups requires careful preparation but can be very lucrative. After delivering an elevator speech or presentation to a small group, you can walk away with leads and sign-ups. The history-of-change model presented in this chapter shows graphically the speed-up of change and how turbulence itself offers opportunity to prospect.

CHAPTER SEVEN
BUILDING YOUR LOYAL TRIBE

The first step in building your fan base is to start building your email distribution list. This list is *the most important document for your business.* Your goal should be to have 100,000 email addresses subscribed to your distribution list. To build up a customer base takes time and dedication. Your emphasis should always be on making your contacts *personal.*

As with coaching itself, marketing yourself is about building relationships. Make yourself visible by attending Chamber of Commerce and other business networking events and collecting business cards. In the days and weeks that follow, send emails to let your new contacts know how much you appreciated meeting them, ask whether you can do anything to support them, and then continue to keep in touch. By building relationships, you establish yourself as a reliable resource and open the door to new opportunities.

Be smart about reaching out. The best place to start is by looking at your existing client base. Ask these customers for referrals. Use the information you've collected about them (zip code, preferred form of payment, average transaction amount, etc.) to build a typical customer profile.

Explore ways to expand your specialized content. Keep updating the information you offer to customers on your website and thinking about how you could provide even more valuable material to potential coaching clients. You might include a form visitors can fill out to receive a free coaching session.

THE IMPORTANCE OF SPECIALIZATION AND PIONEERING

Coaches with general knowledge are a dime a dozen. While some are very successful, most have to fight fiercely to stay afloat due to the incredible amount of competition. By specializing in an area, you can secure a stronger foothold in their market and also boost your income.

Another approach to specialization is being a pioneer. Pioneers blaze new trails. When there is a demand for a new, unreached niche, the income potential can be even higher than being a specialist! The following questions will help you and your clients think more about specialization and pioneering.

- What are three subcategories of your passion in which you can further specialize?
- What are the characteristics of each of these? Who is the target audience for each?
- What do you know about each of these markets?
- What can you learn from resources available to you in each field?

- How much do coaches earn in each area?

- How long a relationship can you expect to have with your clients?

- Who are the biggest competitors in each niche?

- How can you differentiate yourself from them?

GETTING YOUR COACHING BUSINESS UP AND RUNNING

Most people don't have the luxury of jumping directly into becoming a full-time coach. To do so requires enough savings to cover your monthly financial obligations while building up your clientele. As a result, most people maintain their current jobs and start coaching in a part-time capacity until their clientele is built up enough to cover their monthly costs. From there, you will be able to transition to coaching full-time.

To help you break down the factors you need to consider when transitioning into the coaching profession, use this worksheet.

1. Will you coach part time or full time?

2. What are the advantages of that choice?

3. What are the disadvantages?

4. Who are ten people you can offer free coaching services to?

5. How many clients can you afford to take on for free and how much time can you devote to each?

6. Given that amount of time, what is the total market value of the services you can provide?

7.   After establishing rapport, how can the existing free clients be solicited for testimonials?

EMPATHY AND AUTHORITY

By the nature of the position, coaches are viewed as authority figures. Hence, your clients will naturally be susceptible to your influence. Most of the time, this authority is used ethically but sometimes it isn't. For example, when you challenge clients to rethink their limiting beliefs, they may comply because you are an authority figure. If you then provide examples of what you would do, they will likely try to follow your advice.

Coaches must always put their clients first. It is unethical to use your authority to force your will on clients. The better you understand that your goal is to help your clients accomplish their goals, the more your clients will respect you. When empathy and authority go hand in hand, it creates an opportunity in your coaching practice to grow deep relationships while being likeable.

As I've said, one of the best ways to show empathy is to use active listening and repeat back to the person what they told you in your own words. This makes the client feel validated. Beyond that, you need to show your emotion through your words. Feel the emotions they're feeling. This will show that you care.

While you're focusing on their goals and the actions they're taking to accomplish those goals, look for ways you can give your clients positive reinforcement and affirmation. For example, if they say how they took positive action toward their goals four out of seven days, then encourage them for having made progress. Remind them that most people never even start. Let them know they're doing great and encourage them to keep going.

If you notice shortcomings while you're communicating, write them down and address them with your client. When talking about shortcomings, you need to be tactful. A good approach is to first affirm the good in what they've done and then show them their areas of opportunity. Finally, give them recommendations for how to do better in those areas.

After coaching Rob for a few weeks, I had established my role as an authority figure. Opening up a little and making Rob feel comfortable in the environment to express his ideas and what he was most passionate about enabled me to guide him in taking more actions then he would have on his own.

As I mentioned previously, Rob wanted to become a coach so it was easy for me to understand his thoughts, feelings, fears, and questions about whether or not he would be successful. We were able to openly communicate with one another without any boundaries or limits, as Rob was so open and receptive.

You will go through a relationship-building phase with each of your coaching clients. Laying a good, solid foundation in any relationship will allow it to grow in the proper manner. Rob was looking to me for answers and to help him grow in areas where he was not feeling confident about himself. Providing that support and being a strong sounding board really helped him flourish.

COACHING MODEL: Importance of Brain Research in Coaching

Brain research is constantly coming up with results that provide lots of information for coaches. Every day, new findings are published that can help you as a coach to better understand your clients and even provide fresh ideas about how better to work with them.

Research studies surrounding the power of the brain to learn, adapt, and achieve goals are particularly relevant to us as coaches. For example, one recent study compared two groups of subjects, all of whom were familiar with the piano. Both groups were given the task of learning a complicated finger exercise in a brief amount of time. The difference was that while one group practiced the exercise on the piano, the other group only practiced it mentally. That is, they visualized doing the exercise over and over again. When the results were compiled, the group that practiced mentally had developed as much skill as or more than the others!

What does this finding mean for you as a coach? It means that you can be of greater assistance to those clients who are struggling with achieving their goals by showing them that just thinking about a goal, even without doing anything else toward achieving it, is effective. You can share this research with them as part of a discussion about how merely thinking repeatedly about their goal, they can be sure that they are endowing their brains with the capacity to achieve their goal.

Such an approach can be especially effective with clients who are in periods of low motivation or even discouragement. You can share the research and tell them, "I know you're telling me you don't *want* to work so hard at changing but do you want to want to? Just *wanting to want to change* has an effect on your brain cells, in that desired direction."

Many studies show the brain's capacity to strengthening itself through learning. Neuroplasticity, or brain plasticity, refers to the brain's ability to change throughout life. The human brain has the amazing ability to reorganize itself by forming new connections between brain cells (neurons).

In one case, a surgeon in his fifties suffered a stroke that left his left arm paralyzed. During his rehabilitation, his good arm and hand were immobilized and he was assigned the task of cleaning tables. At first the task was impossible. Then slowly the bad arm remembered how to move. In time he learned to write and play tennis again. The functions of the brain areas affected by the stroke had transferred themselves to healthy regions!

PLASTICITY, LEARNING AND MEMORY

You can boost your brainpower at any age. For a long time it was believed that as we aged, the connections in the brain became fixed. Research has shown that in fact the brain never stops changing through learning. Plasticity is the capacity of the brain to change with learning. Changes associated with learning occur mostly at the level of the connections between neurons. New connections can form and the internal structure of the existing synapses can change.

When you become an expert in a specific domain, the areas in your brain that deal with this type of skill will grow. For instance, London taxi drivers have a larger hippocampus (posterior region of the brain) than bus drivers. Why is that? It is because this region of the hippocampus is specialized in acquiring and using complex spatial information in order to navigate efficiently. Taxi drivers have to navigate around London, whereas bus drivers follow a limited set of routes.

Advances in medical technology such as the MRI allow brain research to continue and expand. Suppose your client needs to learn a new language. Plasticity can be observed in the brains of bilinguals. It looks like learning a second language is possible through functional changes in the brain: the left inferior parietal cortex is larger in bilingual brains than in monolingual brains.

Plasticity changes also occur more in musician's brains than in those of nonmusicians. One study compared professional musicians to amateur musicians and nonmusicians. It found that gray matter (cortex) volume was highest in professional musicians, intermediate in amateur musicians, and lowest in nonmusicians in several brain areas involved in playing music: motor regions, anterior superior parietal areas, and inferior temporal areas.

Finally, another study showed that extensive learning of abstract information is also able to trigger some plasticity changes in the brain. The study imaged the brains of German medical students three months before their medical exam and right after the exam and then compared them to the brains of students who were not studying for an exam at the time. The medical students' brains showed learning-induced changes in regions of the parietal cortex as well as in the posterior hippocampus. These regions of the brain are known to be involved in memory retrieval and learning.

KEEPING THE BRAIN HEALTHY

Like muscular strength, memory requires that you consistently maintain it. There are many online brain-training programs available. I encourage you to find one you like and to use it regularly. The more your "work out" your brain, the better you'll be able to process and remember information. Most good brain-training programs target a variety of different capacities such as attention, flexibility, speed, and memory. The best brain exercises break your routine and challenge you to use and develop new brain pathways.

You can advise your clients that their personal habits and routines can either add to or detract from their brain's ability to function at its best. For example, physical exercise helps the brain stay sharp. It increases oxygen to the brain and reduces the risk for disorders that lead to memory loss such as diabetes and cardiovascular disease. Most importantly, exercise plays an important role in neuroplasticity by boosting growth factors and stimulating new neural connections.

Sleep is also fundamental to learning and memory. Research shows that sleep is necessary for memory consolidation with key memory-enhancing activity occurring during the deepest stages of sleep. Memory, creativity, problem-solving abilities, and critical thinking skills are all supported when adults get between seven and a half and nine hours of sleep every night.

In contrast to sleep and exercise, stress is one of the brain's worst enemies. Over time, chronic stress destroys brain cells and damages the region of the brain involved in the formation of new memories and the retrieval of old ones. Studies have also linked stress to memory loss. You've heard that laughter is the best medicine, and that holds true for your brain and memory as well. Listening to jokes activates areas of the brain vital to learning and creativity. As psychologist Daniel Goleman notes in his book Emotional Intelligence, "laughter . . . seems to help people think more broadly and associate more freely."

Just as the body needs fuel, so does the brain. I encourage you to eat a brain-boosting diet based on fruits, vegetables, whole grains, "healthy" fats (such as olive oil, nuts, fish), and lean protein to provide lots of health benefits as well as improved memory.

Here are some coaching questions that pertain here:

- How much do you know about current brain research?

- How is your memory these days? Notice any lapses? Remembering names?

- How much sleep are you getting? How much exercise?

- Are you taking frequent breaks at work? Setting realistic expectations for yourself? Expressing feelings instead of bottling them up?

- How can you find humor in your situation?

- How is your diet helping your thinking process and outcomes?

One of the first things that struck me in working with clients was that each of them had a different way of taking in the questions I asked and the information I shared. Wondering about this, I investigated something called "learning styles." I found it very useful. Knowing about learning styles and how to recognize them in a client gave me insights as to how to work with each one.

Consider integrating personality-based indicators into your coaching as well, such as The Meyers-Briggs Type Indicator test. As you become aware of your clients' preferences, styles of processing information, and ways of thinking about themselves, you can become far more effective.

REINVENT YOURSELF TO WIN

To successfully reinvent yourself, you must learn to embrace change. This means to become a person who looks for change and adapts well. Why do I need to reinvent myself? Why is adapting to change so important? The simple answer is that the world is changing at a pace that makes it mandatory for us to change every year. We have to improve continually and reinvent ourselves by changing so we can always improve the value we offer to our clients.

If you or your coaching clients don't change or reinvent fast enough, you can become irrelevant. In order to be successful, you have to keep up with the changing markets so you can continually serve and add value.

When I used to teach English there were no programs that were easily accessible to learn English in Japan. It was very easy for me to get new clients and to teach them English. Soon, though, several software companies became popular and made it difficult for me to grow my business of teaching English.

Since I wasn't very passionate about teaching, I didn't have a lot of motivation to create any software of my own or write a book on the topic. I could have programmed the software years before my competitors entered the market but I wasn't passionate about the topic. What I cared about was personal growth but the vehicle I was using was serving neither my clients nor me.

What I realized when the competitors arrived was that I didn't have sufficient passion around teaching English to Japanese people. I wasn't reinventing myself or adapting well enough to stay relevant to the market. So software came in and put me out of business.

The best way to change and adapt to different situations is by understanding your market. Read at least two new books about your market each month and gain at least fifteen new relationships with others in your market. This way you can stay on top of the changes and continually grow.

One of the best ways to start with a new client is to ask them how easy change is for them. Ask them if they need to focus on a change growth plan—a plan that outlines how to grow in the area where they most need to change. This plan requires creating lists of areas they can change in and setting goals that you can help them manage as a coach.

I find that people tend to live in their heads when it comes to change. They love to think about a needed change but they never seem to start implementing it. A good method is to ask them what big changes they have helped clients make in the past ten years. Then, figure out what they want to do over the next ten years. From there, put together a list of skills the client feels they need to improve over time. After you've gotten clarity for yourself and your coaching client, the next step is to start the process of change by setting goals.

SMART GOALS

Start by using a basic goal-setting framework called SMART goals. SMART is an acronym for specific, measurable, attainable, realistic, and timely. Let's run through a SMART goal so you can see how it works.

One of my clients, Julia, wanted to lose weight. She said she'd tried everything but never saw any results. I told her about SMART goals and we started by coming up with a specific number—the number of pounds she needed to lose to consider her effort a success. I asked her how much weight she wanted to lose and she told me, "Enough to fit into my old dresses." That took care of the first point: her goal was specific.

Next, we came up a way to measure her progress, like check-in points. To stay on track, she had to lose at least two pounds per week. This standard helped us establish clear accountability.

Then we had to strategize how she would attain the goal. What combination of diet and exercise could she maintain?

Next, we made sure the goal was realistic. Expecting her to lose ten pounds per week looked great on paper, but it would never happen. By contrast, two pounds a week was very possible.

Finally, based on her projected two-pounds-per-week loss, we put a time on the overall goal.

As she progressed, some weeks Julia fell short. Since we kept track of all the results and maintained the two-pounds-per-week standard, she had to work extra hard the following week to make up for it. In the end, Julia achieved her goal three weeks earlier than projected!

By implementing SMART goals, Julia went from no results to mission accomplished!

CHAPTER SUMMARY

Specialization is a way to build your fan base. The more you specialize, the more you can be seen as an expert. Becoming a pioneer by opening up new sub-categories of your passion can also open new markets for you.

Help your clients make decisions about whether to work full or part time, what target markets to focus on, what to charge, etcetera. Being ethical and empathetic go hand in hand with being an authority. Using skillful questions, you can gently confront a client about their negative or self-defeating attitudes.

The explosion of research findings about the way the human brain works should be an area of interest to today's coach. Using the studies, you can get clients interested in and motivated about taking better care of themselves.

Staying on top of change is a key to success today. As a coach you need to constantly be on the lookout for ways to reinvent yourself.

You can help clients by using a model such as SMART goal setting.

CHAPTER EIGHT

OVER DELIVER VALUE TO YOUR COMMUNITY

BUILDING TRUST

I t's hard to imagine, but just over fifty years ago, advertisers could simply make a claim for their product and people would buy it. There was little or no substantiating of the claim, and little demand for it. "This soft drink tastes better." "This soap will wash clothes whiter." "This car will please you more." These kinds of claims still go on, but customers are wiser because they can research anything through search engines, and online products have customer comments.

Building trust is key to success as a coach. So how do you get potential coaching clients to trust you enough to sign up or at least to want to take a free taste? The complimentary session is one way. This is one of the best ways to have potential clients sample your service.

Giving products and services away for free is certainly growing in popularity. You can see the success of this strategy with companies like Google and Facebook. Perhaps the best-known example was Gillette, which, by giving away razors, created the demand for disposable blades. This business model is now the foundation of entire industries: give away the cell phone, sell the monthly plan. Make the videogame console cheap and sell expensive games. Install fancy coffeemakers in offices at no charge so you can sell managers expensive coffee sachets. Will the model continue to be successful? Perhaps the answer is in the title of a widely read article that appeared recently in a popular national magazine: "Free! Why $0.00 Is the Future of Business."

The best freebie is one that costs you little or nothing to produce but delivers measurable results. Giving away an e-book rewards people for joining your mailing list or subscribing to your newsletter and it can generate leads. When you think about offering free coaching, you must see it is a business strategy. The main point is to make sure that this service turns out to be of very high value to the client. If it is, it should result not only in high satisfaction for them but the likelihood they will tell others about your coaching services.

The usual temptation with this model is to stop short of giving real value for fear that if you give away something great, no one will come back to buy. Break that mind-set. In a typical business, the single greatest expense is sales and marketing costs, so offering a free product or service is an extremely smart way to acquire customers at a low cost then monetize them later in a different way.

So how do you use the "free razor blade method" to add value and build trust as a coach? Once you have built up your client base of raving fans, you can keep building trust by giving away content and products.

First, content. Since many of your clients may become coaches themselves, a natural way to build trust is to share your tricks and tools of the trade. They are already picking up a lot about being a coach by working with you but you can answer their technical or skill-related questions as well.

- Do you have any questions?
- Did you notice how that conversation led to your going deeper in your resolve to achieve success? What did you notice I did as your coach do to help make that happen?
- Which questions led you to explore that alternative?

Such promptings can lead to a discussion of your coaching techniques. Another way to demonstrate your goodwill is to refer your clients to coaching books, articles, or online presentations that can help them.

Second, products. As you build your coaching business, you will create products—for example, articles, blog pieces, books, and instructional videos. By giving these away—always discreetly, with an eye to future growth of the client base—you are not only displaying generosity but also indicating to clients that you believe genuinely in their success and are willing to make sacrifices of your own to help.

When I first started coaching, I immediately offered my family and friends free sessions. Thankfully, they were incredibly supportive and most participated.

When I asked them to pay for coaching, things changed. Since most of my relationships were nontransactional relationships, I'd never asked them to pay me for any services before. This made it difficult to transition to a transactional arrangement.

Then I figured out an effective approach: I started asking my closest contacts what excited them most about getting coached and what benefits they got from our sessions. I collected testimonials with their photos. I then asked each of them for a list of friends whom I could call to offer a free coaching session.

Within four weeks of my first coaching sessions with family and friends, I started making the calls. Afterwards, I had over seventeen people sign up for monthly coaching program!

This example shows how your business survives based on people's interest in your services. You're at the mercy of the prospect. Also, the amount of time it takes to get a sustainable full-time business running isn't exact. I myself didn't know it would take a month; I thought it would work right away!

I want to strongly emphasize this point: Before you transition from your present job to full-time coaching or switch your full-time job to part time, you should have sufficient savings to sustain you for six months. Of course, every starting coach's situation is different, so the exact numbers may vary. The only alternative to savings, in my recommendation, would be if you were coaching at least ten clients a week.

If your clients want to become coaches themselves, help them find their niche and ten people they can coach for free. They should record these sessions. Be sure to have them practice their intake session with you before meeting with their first paying clients.

The first step is to coach people for free. How will you get your first ten free clients? Beyond referrals from friends and family, Facebook is another great way to start. Search for groups related to their areas of focus (as in their passion). For example, if you are looking to coach someone in some area pertaining to the environment, seek out those groups on Facebook. From there, start posting to communicate that you are offering free coaching sessions for anyone who is interested. Keep going until you've secured ten free session clients.

If you stick to this approach, you are most likely to see results. In fact, I've never seen anyone fail using this technique. Free coaching sessions are very easy to get. People like free!

TAKING ADVANTAGE OF TECHNOLOGY IN YOUR COACHING SESSIONS

It used to be that coaching was done in person with the coach and client sitting face-to-face in the same room. This meant you could only coach clients you could connect with by driving. Then telephone coaching became the usual way to engage with a client. Email came along to provide a means of scheduling calls, providing interim notifications, or sharing data and recommending websites. Lately, Skype (as well as GoToMeeting and Hangouts) is catching up with the telephone as a preferred method of meeting.

Tips for Using Skype with Clients

Since clients are often happy to go beyond their local area to find the right person, online coaching is becoming popular globally. As coaching grows in popularity, so does the quantity of technology available to increase its effectiveness. Skype is an excellent example of this.

Technology Issues

When you are using online services to conduct coaching sessions such as Skype, GoToMeeting, or Google Hangouts, you might experience some initial concern or complications. It can help if you develop backup plans, such as informing your clients that problems with the audio or visual connections might take place and what to do if either of you start to experience them. Some of the steps I take to reduce the chances of technical issues disrupting my coaching calls are the following.

1. Practice handling the technology in advance

Whenever you're trying out an online service for the first time, practice with a family member first to make sure everything is in order before you need to use it with a client. When you set up the initial client meeting, provide a plan to call their phone number if the audio or picture goes out. Once they become a client, you will probably continue to use either Skype or another video mode of conferencing.

2. Help the client see you

Since more than half of all communication is delivered through body language, make sure your upper body is included in the video image, not just your face. This way, clients can see any hand gestures you make and your body language. If possible, have a fairly blank, noncluttered background behind you. Keep the environment as professional as possible. Also, never hesitate to ask your client how they felt the coaching session went, since that can open the lines of communication and provide feedback to continually improve future sessions.

3. Connect with your client

Look directly into the camera on your computer, not the screen, to ensure eye contact is maintained. If you are distracted by things on your desk or are looking at unrelated items on your computer while talking, this will give the impression that you are trying to do other things during the coaching session and can anger or annoy your client, adversely affecting your reputation as a coach. Whenever you are on camera, accentuate your enthusiasm, active listening skills, smiling, and hand gestures so they are obvious to the client.

4. Cut out distractions

Decrease distractions to you and your clients during calls. Interruptions can be embarrassing and annoying to the client. Before starting each Skype coaching call, remember to put your home and mobile phones on silent, shut down any distracting applications or email notifications on your computer, and keep all pets out of sight.

5. Draw diagrams

Being able to draw diagrams to make key points with your clients can enhance sessions by providing a break from looking at each other. If you are using an Apple computer, an app called Paper53 is available and free and allows you to draw, sketch, or write down notes. Another app called Reflector Director can be used to reflect the images you create using Paper53 onto your computer screen. This allows your client to view the sketch as you're drawing it.

"THE VALUE YOU GIVE COMES BACK TO YOU."

AKIRA IGUCHI

TOOLS OF THE TRADE

Your laptop and smartphone are the two most important pieces of hardware you will use in your coaching business. A good tablet counts, too, for it's like taking your computer with you. Beyond the usual features and your search engines, I recommend that you install the following apps: Skype, Evernote, Chrome, Tweetbot, Pomodoro Timer, and Google Docs.

As for your cell phone, it should have the same applications plus Basecamp 3 and a good microphone and camera. Always keep an eye out for great new productivity apps and don't be afraid to try out new applications that could save you time, money, or organizational headaches.

HOW TO CHARGE CLIENTS

Especially in the beginning, you may need help determining how to charge for your services. You may struggle with the idea of working for free. But remember it's the best way to prove value, establish a good reputation, and earn solid testimonials.

Once those bases are covered, you'll be able to start charging and building your brand. When you are established, you will need to know how to increase your rates in a way that won't cause you to lose clients. Here are some questions to guide your approach:

1. What are the reasons why it's important that you offer your services for free when starting out?

2. When you start charging, what is the lowest rate you're willing to charge?

3. How many clients at your low rate do you need to meet your minimum financial goals?

4. What's the highest rate you would charge a client?

5. How many clients at your highest rate do you need to meet your minimum financial goals?

6. Now it's time to establish threshold ranges for each rate. How much additional value can you provide that will allow you to charge more at each stage?

COACHING MODEL: Control or Surrender?

In white-water kayaking there is a rule called "dip on the crest." When you are in a small boat on a turbulent river, you are going up and down. Sometimes you are up high on the crest of a wave and then in a matter of seconds you are deep in the trough between waves, hidden from sight by the mountains of white water. Experienced paddlers know to save their energy by dipping their paddles only when it can make a difference.

You don't have to paddle to go down the river. The river's flow takes care of that. Paddling is best used to make constant, small directional adjustments to keep the boat parallel with the river. The times you need to use your paddle are when you are in danger of capsizing.

Whenever the boat is in a trough with its ends in the water, no amount of paddling can move it. An experienced paddler will therefore hold his or her paddle out of the water. On the other hand, when the boat is atop a wave, the paddle can be dipped to correct direction. Also, the kayaker has a clear view downstream in those moments.

All this gives rise to the strategy of *dipping on the crest*. As a coach, you can use the same principle with clients. That is, many clients will exhaust themselves trying to make a change when circumstances are such that the "boat ends are in the water." In other words, opposing forces are in charge. You can coach the client in such a situation to just "hold the paddle up" and "ride the river," looking for the next wave crest to "dip" (leverage the next opportunity).

The song "The Gambler" by Kenny Rogers contains the following lyrics: "You've got to know when to hold 'em / Know when to fold 'em / Know when to walk away / And know when to run." One of the secrets of living successfully in a crazy world is to achieve and maintain a balance, both in work and in life, between making things happen and letting things happen.

In their quest for success, more and more people are emphasizing aggressiveness and control to such an extent that it is difficult for them to take the pressure off—or even to imagine a reason for doing so. When it comes to preserving balance and perspective, though, overcontrol can be a liability. Happy, productive people are balanced. They know about surrender and they know about control. With them, it's all a matter of timing. As change speeds up, these folks surf the tides. Like whitewater paddlers, they know when to dip the paddle and when to enjoy the ride.

COACHING STRATEGY: CONTROL OR SURRENDER?

How can you help your clients develop an inner edge? Here is a simple exercise that may help them discover more balance, quickly. To do it, they need an "item"—a current problem they are facing or an area where they are experiencing dissatisfaction. Advise them to take the following steps:

1. Write down a description of the item in one short phrase.

2. Sit quietly. Relax, and close your eyes. Spend thirty seconds concentrating on the issue you wrote down. Then let it go.

3. Become aware of your breathing without changing it. Observe the breath as if it is that of another person.

4. Alternate several fifteen-second periods of breathing with "being breathed." In the latter case, pretend the air is breathing you. Then return to control breathing, where you clearly feel yourself as the breather. Switch back and forth several times between control breathing and surrender breathing, studying the feelings associated with each mode.

5. Open your eyes and look back at your issue. Identify which list of feelings connects more strongly with the way you have been addressing the problem.

6. Consider practicing the other kind of approach. For example, if you have been trying to control the problem, think about surrendering more to it. What advantages might it bring? What does it have to teach you? How

can you leverage it or cooperate with it? If you have been surrendering to the problem, consider controlling it more. What resources could you muster up for an attack? Who could you tell or ask about it? What are the steps of an action plan?

7. If you have been more surrendering in dealing with the issue, either avoiding it or thinking you have few or no options, make a list of ways to bring more muscle onto it. Do research. Think about times you have been more forceful. What did you do that worked? Speak up. Assert yourself. Let people know where you stand, while asking for their ideas or help.

GETTING TESTIMONIALS

When you start your coaching sessions, keep in mind that you want to get a photo and a written testimonial about their experience. Ask your clients in advance if they could provide a testimonial and a paragraph about their experience if they like the coaching session. This helps in two ways. First, it eliminates awkward postsession requests. Second, when people know they are giving you something in exchange for the free coaching session, they will feel more at ease and committed to the process.

Here are a few things to remember about testimonials: they are very important to starting a successful coaching practice. Always seek out testimonials, especially focused on how your clients got results from working with you.

Clients who work in a specific niche are often looking for a coach who is the expert in that field. Or they are shopping for a specialist in their particular issue area. When you build your coaching business on your own passion, the area of most consuming interest to you, you have the benefit of attracting these clients because you can often share your own story of overcoming their issue. This builds credibility and attachment to you as a potential coach.

The fact that you are building your Lifestyle Millionaire Coaching business around your passion makes providing value for your clients a natural outcome. Most share your passion and will want to "pick your brain" from time to time.

As soon as I had an email list of a thousand or more, I asked myself: How can I produce products these and other clients will want and buy? As I began to answer that question, I came to see the value of giving some of those products away. Occasionally I offered free coaching or free seminars. The offer of something free was like magic for clients who already liked what I did and me.

In time I made it a standard practice to give away a thirty- or forty-minute video for free, as a gesture of goodwill to my fans or subscribers. I discovered right away that this built trust. My clients began to look upon me as an expert in the coaching and seminar industry. What's more, it created a comfort level that allowed my subscribers to become my consumers. I found in time that I was constantly producing things to offer them free of charge. It was great marketing outside of my list and word would get out of people saying, "Do you know what Akira did for me? . . . And he didn't even charge me for it! . . . Yes, you can get in on it, too! Just sign up!"

CHAPTER SUMMARY

Fans are people who know about and are interested in you, whether or not they are clients. A common but always useful way to build your fan base is the "free taste." Figure out how to give away something of great value to others that is of little expense for you to create. This can be tricky because people are savvy. At the same time, they like free stuff. So make sure you add value, whether it is a free coaching session, an online article, or referring fans to a useful resource. You need to keep thinking of products you can offer. The online fan base is hungry for new ideas, tips, and free things to acquire.

The start-up coach needs to plan wisely. It will be a while before you are earning appreciable from your coaching, and it may never take the place of your job. In any case, start offering complimentary coaching sessions and using each session to build leads and referrals. Asking a person you have coached for a testimonial is a good way to get a return on a free session, even if they can't refer someone else to you.

Skype is the way many coaches conduct their sessions. Follow the steps for making a professional impression offered in this chapter. Some coaches do pretty much all their business through a smartphone.

Be smart about setting your rates. Depending on your following, you can increase your fees.

The control-or-surrender model offers a framework for coaching. You can support people in making efforts when it counts (dipping on the crest) and not wasting efforts when they can't make a difference.

CHAPTER NINE

CREATE YOUR IRRESISTIBLE OFFER

reate the base. Build trust. Make the offer. That's the Lifestyle Millionaire Coaching process to win clients. Sounds easy, and it is, provided that you work hard at the first two steps. After establishing trust by letting your fan base get to know you through your email broadcasts, social media, and free content, it is time to make an offer. With confidence as an expert, you are now in a place to ask your fan base to buy your product or services.

THE IRRESISTIBLE OFFER

What makes an irresistible offer? An irresistible offer has a financial component to it, which is where I suggest you start. You need to ask the question: what do I have to offer in this coaching session to make this a no-brainer purchase? And, what promises do I have to make that will make this offer resistible?

I remember making this offer: "I will help you build a business around your passion. In the next twelve months you will not only have a successful coaching practice built around your passion but also you will love your work and make a great living from it."

That kind of offer allowed people to see actual, tangible results in their minds. I knew when I made it that they would put a great value on it. I needed to make sure that in their minds, they were at least breaking even in the amount of ten times what they paid me. It was a strong offer, promising strong results. It also required a strong commitment on my part. To be sure, I had to hold up my end.

BUILDING A GENIUS TEAM

Once you get a team together, beyond making sure they are working well, focus on how people are treated. Do they see themselves as employees or as partners? Do you pay well? Offer bonuses? Offer shares or profit-sharing? This is not just economics; it has to do with how people feel valued.

Remember when my staff unexpectedly quit on me? Passion can be strengthened through adversity. We all have our ways of learning what we need to learn. Mine seems to be by disaster. I will be going along, thinking everything is fine, and suddenly be blindsided by something like that—being "fired" by my team. As usual, I started out feeling like a victim. How could they do that? Why does this happen to me? Etc.

But then—still in keeping with my preferred method of learning something I need to know—I sat down and started asking the right questions, ones that follow the adage "Change yourself and you can change others." For example, how did I contribute to this? How could I have prevented it? How could it be fixed? What can I do to make sure it doesn't happen again?

I did some serious thinking about that last question and decided I would behave very differently once I had a new team together. How did I do that? First of all, I tried to go after people who were great, if not the best, at what they did. For example, were they incredible at marketing, event management, technology, writing, or managing and growing the fan base?

Beyond that, I was careful to share my mission, passion, and values with each person during their recruitment. I shared about my personal life, values, and where I wanted to go. I asked them about those same things as well. In other words, my recruiting meetings went very much like an intake coaching session.

Realizing I had let my old team down by being out of touch, I decided that, as in coaching, communication was key. When I did pull a very able team together, I made sure that I stayed in touch with them not just by phone or email but also through occasional dinners or fun events. I made myself visible and available. I listened to them. I celebrated their gifts and accomplishments. I made them the stars.

Make sure you talk often with your team members about where you are going, what the goal is, what the purpose of each event, speech, or book is and how it serves the mission. Keep reminding them that this business is all about making a difference in people's lives, including their own! Remember this:

People who do good work feel good about themselves and
people who feel good about themselves do good work.

On your website, you should set up a video, landing page, and sign-up subscription form. You should be able to readily add examples and templates. Also, be sure to watch "10 Laws of Social Media Marketing" by visiting http://www.entrepreneur.com/article/218160.

COACHING MODEL: Helping Clients Train Their Intuition

Momentary balance between the control and surrender forces enables us to use the rod of intuition to know answers perfectly and immediately—without necessarily knowing how we know them. We are not looking at things; we are *feeling* them from within, with instant, effortless, deep understanding. By this means we not only transcend the hurry-up, we make more time.

You can help your client train his or her balance and intuitive functioning like an athlete through management of attention. Anecdotes from sports figures such as being "in the zone" can enrich our understanding, connecting that extraordinary functioning with our own experience. For example, Bill Russell of the Boston Celtics—the basketball team that won ten NBA championships in thirteen years—described the experience of perfect attention and response this way:

"Every so often a Celtic game would heat up so that it became magical. When it happened, I could feel my play rise to a new level. Three or four plays were not enough to get it going. It would surround not only me and the other Celtics, but also the players on the other team and even the referees. At that special level, all sorts of odd things happened. The game would be in a white heat of competition—which is a miracle in itself—yet I never felt the pain. The game would be surprising, yet nothing could surprise me.

"It was almost as if we were playing in slow motion. I could almost sense how the next play would develop and where the next shot would be taken. Even before the other team brought the ball in bounds, I could feel it so keenly that I'd want to shout to my teammates, "It's coming there!" except that that I knew that everything would change if I did. My premonitions would be consistently correct, and I always felt then that I not only knew all the Celtics by heart, but also all the opposing players, and that they all knew me.

"These were moments when I had chills pulsing up and down my spine. Sometimes the feeling would last all the way to the end of the game. On the occasions when the game ended at that special level, I literally did not care who had won. If we lost, I'd still be as free and as high as a skyhawk."

We've all tuned in at times to a level that is almost magical, where we feel our play rise to a new level, where we have all the time in the world because things seem to move in slow motion. Nothing surprises us. We can sense what will develop before it happens, then watch our premonitions play out. In an extraordinary way we are tuned in to the environment—our own people, the competition, customers. We seem to know them all by heart and to be known by them. In this heightened consciousness we don't care about the score. Whatever way the game comes out, we are "free and high as a skyhawk."

Currently intuition, which once seemed limited to random "hunches" that came true, is undergoing scrutiny. In fact, with the constant speed of change, your clients are required to make on-the-spot decisions without the time to search for answers. Be open to helping your clients become intuition-focused "players." Intuition scores high these days as an executive skill. Companies are looking for leaders who can trust their own instincts when decision making in the absence of supporting data is needed.

MINIMIZING STARTUP COSTS

We all want to make more money so we can enjoy our life, not buy more capital! I've been coaching for years and I don't even own a printer. I do almost all my coaching on my cell phone and a good Wi-Fi connection. I have invested in headphones that have noise cancellation in the microphone. I highly recommend you do the same to maintain your professionalism while coaching in noisy environments, which come up far more frequently than you'd think!

A great aspect of the Lifestyle Millionaire Coaching business model is the low startup costs. In fact, here are some things you do not need to purchase: a desk, a computer, a special chair, a printer, printer paper, office space, or business cards.

With the right smartphone, a great data and service plan, and a notebook, you are almost in business. Smartphones with larger screens can be used not only as a means of communicating with clients and affiliates but also for taking notes, conference calls, and scheduling, if you like.

Some phones allow you to connect over Wi-Fi, meaning you won't be charged for minutes you use on your phone plan. For example, on recent iPhone versions you can switch to Wi-Fi mode and make calls. Regardless of the smartphone you have, as long as you have Skype, you can talk over Wi-Fi.

Make sure you get familiar with your data plan's availability in your area so you can best advise your coaching clients on what plans best meet their needs. They'll love you for saving them the time and effort to do this research and even more for finding them a plan where they don't end up paying for overages.

As you progress with your coaching clients, make sure they can text, email, Skype/Facetime/Google Talk, Facebook, and Twitter from their phones. For now make sure they get the right phone, with the right data package—and be sure the phone allows for apps.

Let's talk about saving money on software. Believe it or not, most of the free versions of software are better than their paid alternatives. For example, you don't need to go out and buy Microsoft Office. Google Docs, Google Sheets, and Google Slides are free alternatives that can work for you and your coaching clients. What's especially great about these free apps is that all of the documents are stored on the associated Google account so they can be accessed anywhere via your Internet connection!

Make sure you have a Gmail account. I also suggest creating an Evernote account. This will allow you to take notes on each of your clients and keep them neatly organized. Beyond that, it has some powerful capturing and sharing features.

Now you don't need all of the expensive equipment generally associated with starting a business! Welcome to the Lifestyle Millionaire approach!

CHAPTER SUMMARY

Once you have built your fan base, you can make an irresistible offer. Craft your promise well so that the results are tangible and make a strong commitment to follow through on it.

If you build a team, make them feel like stars. Share your dreams and failures with them, let them get to know you as a person, and spend time with them away from the office. Stay in touch with each team member not just to discuss work but also personal matters. Find out the things that mean the most to them and ask about them. Your investment in your team will result in their doing better work, sharing your mission, and staying with you through the best and worst times.

A virtually untapped resource in each of us is intuition. Like a muscle, the intuition needs to be trained. Learn to rely on feeling. Trust and follow your hunches and teach clients to follow theirs.

Show your clients they can operate their businesses with simplicity, keeping costs low by not purchasing unneeded equipment.

CHAPTER TEN

BEGINNING OF YOUR NEW JOURNEY

This morning I received an email from a man in Korea that moved me. In hopes that it might inspire you as well, I share it with you here:

Dear Akira Iguchi,

I just read your book Thinking Poor, Thinking Rich for the third time. I will read it five times more. Your book has not only changed my thinking, it has changed my life. I want to become everything you wrote about in this book, to pattern my thinking and my actions around it. I want to be a teacher like you, and help others like you are doing. Can you come to Korea to do a seminar soon? I would like to help you make contacts to set it up. Thank you for what you have done for me.

Signed, _____

I felt so touched and happy as I read this letter. I found myself imagining this man, who lived far away and whom I did not know, picking up my book and getting excited and inspired as he read it. I wondered what he would do now and how, motivated by something I had written, he would go out and make something better of his life.

I'm asking myself today, how was I so fortunate as to have this kind of impact on an individual like this man?

But I didn't always feel this so deeply. This communication is like much of the feedback I've received over the years from my 100,000 online contacts; it has been grateful, but it didn't always thrill me and make me so grateful. It was not always like this.

In 2013, after completing a 150-day push by holding a huge life seminar and asking, as usual, "Now what?" it hit me. I was burned out.

I had been keeping up a total go-go-go lifestyle. While the thrill of success was still there, it was not sustainable. I had plenty of money and fun but somehow I had not acknowledged myself. My body and mind were under constant stimulation and excitement. What about my heart, feelings, and spirit?

Like all the people I had been serving in my coaching, blogging, speaking, and training, I needed love. I needed connectedness.

All the money-making and scurrying around, climbing to the heights in my business, and becoming an acknowledged leader in my profession had not fulfilled me. I needed "something more." My passion had been teaching, training, and showing others how to connect. What about feeling connection in my own life?

I had been hearing all about the "mindfulness revolution" taking place in the U.S. It seemed right down my alley, since I had always been the Inner Game guy.

Mindfulness books and seminars were available, so I attended and learned how to meditate. That began a practice that I have carried out daily from that time—right up to and including this morning when I received the letter from the man in Korea.

Very soon after beginning to meditate, I felt more peaceful, centered, and concentrated. My mind wasn't jumping all around, always thinking, "What's next?" before I was even done with what I was doing.

I thought, Wow, this is powerful! How can just ten minutes a day of meditating make me feel more like myself? That's when I realized, that's what my go-go-go lifestyle had neglected.

The peacefulness was the beginning but there were other results from my newfound practice. I seemed to have a laser-like focus and suddenly felt conscious.

The world of others opened up to me and I realized that I was connected with everyone. Everywhere I looked, I saw that my passion connected me with others and their passions. I saw that everyone else had the need that I had. They wanted to be loved and to feel connected to others but they didn't know how. Now, more than ever, I wanted to help them find out.

What happened to me can be summed up by the word *consciousness*. Back in my childhood memories of Japan, I remembered everyone on the streets looking bored and dull. The few I came across who were lively in spirit, truly excited about their day, and looking forward to what would happen stood out from the crowd.

What I know now is that people can appear lifeless because they are unconscious. They think only about themselves, their own little world and what happens inside it. Millions and millions of people seldom lift their head and look around to even become aware of others, much less interested in them. What they don't realize is that if they were to do this, they wouldn't be down, dreary, and bored all the time. The world would open up to them, as it has to me.

My new question in life was: How can I help others become conscious?

COACHING MODEL: Mindfulness

"Between stimulus and response there's a space; in that space lies our power to choose our response; in our response lies our growth and our freedom."

—Viktor Frankl

If your mind is also running around, seemingly unstoppable, you should know that is a very old condition. For thousands of years, Buddhists have called it "monkey mind," describing the way your attention seems to jump around like a monkey that can't stop leaping among the branches of a tree.

When does your brain get to rest and enjoy the moment? Every morning you wake up and hit the ground running, go-go-go all day trying to keep ahead, and fall exhausted into bed that night, only to wake up and start it all over again. This combination of mental, emotional, and physical fatigue becomes a vicious cycle, often leading to deep feelings of unhappiness and inadequacy.

The very distractions and obligations of modern life are the reason the practice of Mindfulness is taking off so fast. Some are calling it the Mindfulness Revolution. People need to get their crazy lives back on track and they don't know where to start. In other words, they need to live "mindfully."

Mindfulness is actually a pretty simple practice to learn. There are many different ways to do it, such as mindful breathing, mindful eating, mindfulness meditation, walking meditation, etcetera. If you continue practicing mindfulness, every part of your life will be impacted positively—work, relationships, health, creativity.

Mindfulness is the practice of maintaining a nonjudgmental state of awareness of one's thoughts, emotions, or experiences on a moment-to-moment basis. Jon Kabat-Zinn, founder of MSBR (mindfulness-based stress reduction) says: "Mindfulness means paying attention in a particular way: on purpose, in the present moment, and non-judgmentally."

My own interpretation of mindfulness is something you do on purpose, as often as you can remember to do it, and without beating yourself up when you don't. I've found the benefits to include: not being regretful about the past, not worrying about the future, and letting yourself off the hook more when you goof up. That last point—no self-blame—is essential. If you're self-critical about it, meditation simply won't work. Simply observe. The practice of mindfulness is really about learning how to see the good in your life.

Here are some specific practices for mindfulness: Leaving your cell phone in the other room while having dinner at home. Paying attention to how your feet feel when they hit the ground, the feel of the breeze, and the blue of the sky. Being fully present in a work meeting by not letting your mind wander. Really hearing what others say in conversations and making eye contact with them.

When does mindfulness practice pay off? Besides feeling, sleeping, and eating better, you may enjoy life more. For example, say somebody at work or home drops the ball. Momentarily you feel your heart speed up and anger start to boil up. Without mindfulness, you might yell at the person, who responds defensively and a shouting match ensues. Remember that space between stimulus and response? Mindfulness training can help you recognize your stress reactions and modify them.

There is far more to this subject than I can cover here, but mindfulness books, videos, audio programs, and seminars abound. As a coach in this day and age, you need to know not just *about* mindfulness, but how to practice it.

CONSCIOUSNESS AND THE COACH

After you begin your own practice of mindfulness in earnest, you can become a mindfulness coach. You can choose to educate yourself and work under that banner or simply add the techniques and understandings of mindfulness to the way you presently coach people. Either way, here are some questions you can ask a prospect as a mindfulness coach:

- What people or events trigger feelings of stress or anxiety for you?
- How do you react when you feel stress or anxiety?
- Are there particular times of day when you feel you have less control over your feelings and reactions?
- How much sleep are you getting?

- How and when are you eating?

- Tell me about a time when you reacted badly to something and wished you'd acted differently.

- How much time do you spend regretting things from the past?

- How often do you worry about the future?

Such exploration with a client can be useful, whether or not they take you up on supporting them in becoming a practitioner.

MEDITATION

I've already said that meditation makes a difference in my life. There are many forms of meditation—transcendental meditation, yoga, etcetera. I'm not recommending any certain kind, but mindfulness meditation certainly works for me. The purpose of mindfulness meditation is to help train your brain to let go of stress, anxiety, and worry. I learned that its benefits include lowering blood pressure, relieving tension-based pain, reducing anxiety attacks, boosting moods, and strengthening your immune system. You can boil that down to just feeling calmer.

There are actually a variety of mindfulness meditation techniques which you can learn about through reading or attending a class. Central to pretty much all forms of sitting meditation are the following:

- Set a timer for five or ten minutes.

- If you're on a cushion, sit with legs comfortably crossed. If in a chair, let your feet flat on the floor.

- Sit up straight, with the spine erect but relaxed.

- Keep the upper arms parallel to the body, hands in the lap. Don't lean forward.

- Eyes can be closed or open. Many people say that gently raising the gaze to the point between the eyebrows keeps you alert so you don't fall asleep.

- Focus on your breathing, simply observing it as if it were that of another person. Make no attempt to regulate it. Let it "breathe you."

- Whenever your mind wanders, bring it back to the breath without judgment, just observation.

Recently I was in London, traveling on the underground (subway). I noticed again how, at each point of entry or exit of the cars, the sign appeared underfoot: MIND THE GAP. This is a way of warning you to be careful not to misstep and stick your foot between the car and the edge of the platform. I think the phrase can sum up an important point about coaching as well. Your knowledge and practice of mindfulness practices can help you and your clients to "mind the gap" between emotion and action. Mindfulness, as the word implies, means being aware of what you are thinking and feeling, so that you can regulate these functions. Not by repression—just keeping the lid on—but by taking care of your inner self and preserving a sense of balance, what some call "equanimity."

At this point you might be asking, "Why, Akira, here at the end of a book with the word 'millionaire' in the title (presumably because you're saying I can become wealthy through the coaching business you've described), are you talking about such a 'soft' subject as mindfulness?"

The answer is because I've come full circle myself. As I told you, it's easy to become so focused on your next success that you lose your balance, your sense of rightfulness with yourself. You and I know that there are plenty of millionaires out there who don't care anything about others' happiness, except perhaps that of their own loved ones. All they want is more, yet despite all their toys they're not happy. I could have more, but I want what I have. The gratefulness I feel today in receiving such a kind letter is a gift I would not do without.

That's the delusion, I found out. We often think that money and the stuff it buys will satisfy us. My final word in this book is: Don't believe it.

Make sure in your coaching that not only do you prosper yourself, you make a difference in the lives and fortunes of others. Because, as I've said again and again, that is the deepest satisfaction. Without being able to feel your connectedness to others, you could become a starving millionaire—full of materials but hungry for fulfillment. Find your connectedness by helping others connect. Find your success by helping others succeed. Find your love by making others feel loved.

CHAPTER SUMMARY

As I have tried to emphasize throughout this book, a Lifestyle Millionaire Coaching business is a priceless way to prosper. You are simultaneously capitalizing on an opportunity to help people solve their problems and bringing dignity and fulfillment to their lives.

A wealth of communications technology is at your fingertips that can enable you to start a business without an office, employees, or even a desk. There are a host of coaching models and strategies to be learned and used as well.

With your every expenditure of energy, you are benefiting others in a significant way. The payoffs, both financial and emotional, can be huge.

But only if you remain conscious. Especially with everyone around you running after material things, it can be tempting to emphasize material rewards over service, but balancing both tangible and intangible rewards is a secret of making yourself happy. Unless you purposely keep your emotional and spiritual well-being in the forefront, it's easy to live on a treadmill of making money and starving the soul.

Mindfulness, staying aware of your inner life and values through actual practice, will enrich your life and work, and that of your clients. Practicing mindfulness as a way of life can help you reduce stress and control your emotions. Your mind will be more concentrated and you will be able to measure your reactions rather than automatically reacting when setbacks occur. Meditation can be a priceless tool for maintaining a peaceful attitude. Like other mindfulness techniques, it works to help you realize your connectedness to all others and builds fulfillment into whatever tasks you are doing.

Morgan James makes all of our titles available
through the Library for All Charity Organization.

www.LibraryForAll.org